BIBLICAL HEBREW VOCABULARY

BY

CONCEPTUAL CATEGORIES

BIBLICAL HEBREW VOCABULARY

BY

CONCEPTUAL CATEGORIES

A STUDENT'S GUIDE TO NOUNS IN THE OLD TESTAMENT

J. David Pleins

with Jonathan Homrighausen

ZONDERVAN®

ZONDERVAN

Biblical Hebrew Vocabulary by Conceptual Categories
Copyright © 2017 by J. David Pleins

Requests for information should be addressed to:
Zondervan, 3900 Sparks Dr. SE, Grand Rapids, Michigan 49546

ISBN 978-0-310-53074-9

Cover design: Tobias Design: Outerwear for books
Cover photo: Adobe Stock
Interior design: Matthew Van Zomeren

Printed in the United States of America

HB 06.02.2022

J. D. P.: To Hoy Ledbetter†, who first inspired my interest
in biblical languages, his devoted wife Jary and, of course,
to Karen whose friendship, love, and support have brought such joy to my life.

כִּי־עַזָּה כַמָּוֶת אַהֲבָה קָשָׁה כִשְׁאוֹל קִנְאָה
Song of Solomon 8:6b

J. H.: To Michelle and April

אֵשֶׁת־חַיִל מִי יִמְצָא וְרָחֹק מִפְּנִינִים מִכְרָהּ
בָּטַח בָּהּ לֵב בַּעְלָהּ וְשָׁלָל לֹא יֶחְסָר
גְּמָלַתְהוּ טוֹב וְלֹא־רָע כֹּל יְמֵי חַיֶּיהָ
Proverbs 31:10–12

מוֹשִׁיבִי עֲקֶרֶת הַבַּיִת אֵם־הַבָּנִים שְׂמֵחָה הַלְלוּ־יָהּ
Psalm 113:9

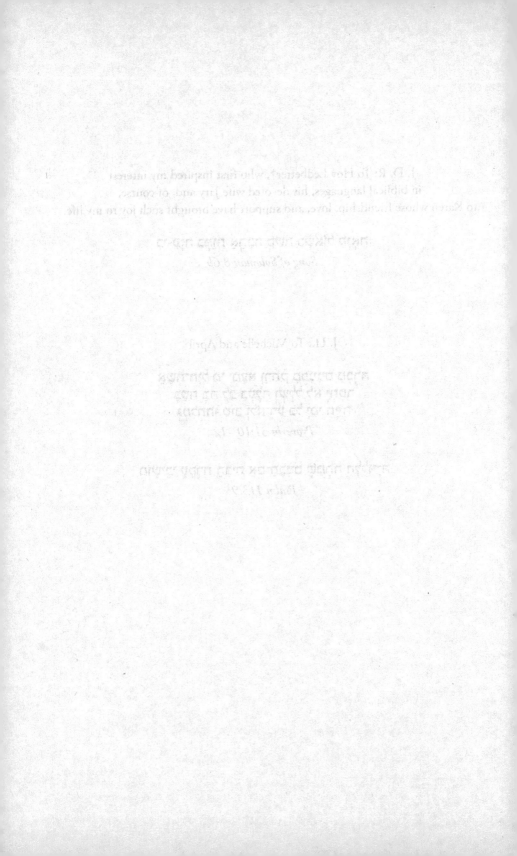

BRIEF TABLE OF CONTENTS

DETAILED TABLE OF CONTENTS

ABBREVIATIONS

CHB   Shafer-Elliott, Cynthia. "Cooking in the Hebrew Bible." *Bible and Interpretation*, May 2013. http://www.bibleinterp.com/articles/2013/sha378013.shtml.

CT   Brenner, Athalya. *Colour Terms in the Old Testament.* Journal for the Study of the Old Testament Supplement Series 21. Sheffield, UK: Sheffield Academic Press, 1982.

DCH   Clines, David J. A, ed. *The Dictionary of Classical Hebrew.* Sheffield: Sheffield Phoenix Press, 1993–2011.

ELT   Borowski, Oded. *Every Living Thing: Daily Use of Animals in Ancient Israel.* Walnut Creek, CA: AltaMira Press, 1999.

FAJ   Shafer-Elliott, Cynthia. *Food in Ancient Judah: Domestic Cooking in the Time of the Hebrew Bible.* BibleWorld. Sheffield, UK: Routledge, 2013.

HALOT   Holladay, William L., ed. *A Concise Hebrew and Aramaic Lexicon of the Old Testament.* Grand Rapids: Eerdmans, 1972.

HCW   Stadelmann, Luis I. J. *The Hebrew Conception of the World: A Philological and Literary Study.* Analecta Biblica 39. Rome: Pontificial Biblical Institute, 1970.

MPTOT   Scott, R. B. Y. "Meteorological Phenomena and Terminology in the Old Testament." *Zeitschrift für die Alttestamentliche Wissenschaft* 64, no. 1 (1952): 11–25.

SDBH   United Bible Societies. *Semantic Dictionary of Biblical Hebrew.* 2000–2009. http://www.sdbh.org/dictionary/main.php?language=en.

UBS   United Bible Societies. *Fauna and Flora of the Bible.* Helps for Translators. London: United Bible Societies, 1980.

כלי   De Moore, Johannes, ed. כלי *Database: Utensils in the Hebrew Bible.* Het Oudstestamentisch Werkgezelschap, 2010–2016. http://www.otw-site.eu/KLY/kly.php.

PREFACE

A command of Hebrew vocabulary is the essential key to an enjoyable encounter with sacred Scripture. Yet beginners who master the basics soon realize that their limited word stock stands in the way of fluid reading and an intuitive grasp of the biblical text. What should be enjoyable exercises in reading Scripture, unmediated by translation, become tedious page-flipping exercises through lexicons. No one tool provides the answer to this frustration. The eager student needs many vocabulary-building resources: Biblical Hebrew word frequency books,[1] Hebrew-English lexicons, a copy of *A Reader's Hebrew Bible* with marginal glosses,[2] flash cards, and perhaps a biblical vocabulary app or two. What makes *Biblical Hebrew Vocabulary by Conceptual Categories (BHVCC)* unique among all these resources is that words are grouped into logical categories. This approach is crucial because the mind constructs its mental space for language by making connections between words. Without these associations, vocabulary building is reduced to rote memorization that all too often becomes an exercise in futility. Unfortunately, until this book was compiled there was no handy reference that brought together all the Hebrew words for items such as gems, trees, birds, weapons, idols, storms, and the like.[3] To be sure, there are a few volumes that cover specific word groups, such as the plants or animals of the Bible, but these books are often limited in scope, cumbersome to use, expensive, and usually only available to those who have access to a specialized theological library (some of the more important titles are listed in the bibliography here). Needless to say, the student requires a more comprehensive and user-friendly resource. At last, in one place, are gathered the words for the body's anatomy, soldiers, ships, musical instruments, celestial phenomena, and more.

Format of *BHVCC*

This work has been divided into four major sections:

- The Created Order
- The Human Order
- The Social Order
- The Constructed Order

---

1. Larry Mitchel, *A Student's Vocabulary for Biblical Hebrew and Aramaic, Updated Edition* (Grand Rapids: Zondervan, 2017); Miles V. Van Pelt and Gary D. Pratico, *The Vocabulary Guide to Biblical Hebrew* (Grand Rapids: Zondervan, 2003); George M. Landes, *Building Your Biblical Hebrew Vocabulary: Learning Words by Frequency and Cognate*, 2nd ed. (Atlanta: Society of Biblical Literature, 2001).
2. A. Philip Brown II and Bryan W. Smith, eds., *A Reader's Hebrew Bible* (Grand Rapids: Zondervan, 2008).
3. While there is a student handbook to New Testament Greek vocabulary by categories, there is no counterpart in English for Old Testament vocabulary. Mark Wilson and Jason Oden, *Mastering New Testament Greek Vocabulary Through Semantic Domains* (Grand Rapids: Kregel Academic, 2003).

Underneath each of these four orders are numerous categories and subcategories designed to group specific meanings and create logical connections. Thus, for example, under "The Created Order," the reader will find the category "Heavens and Earth" with many subcategories such as "Moon" and "Clouds." Under "The Social Order," one finds the category "Family and Kinship" with such subcategories as "Immediate Family" and "Widowhood." Elsewhere, under "The Constructed Order," the student finds, for example, the numerous types of "Containers and Implements," all subdivided into logical groupings such as "Cup," "Pans," and "Cutting Implements." In short, the entire book is carefully arranged to create sensible groupings of related terms.

Each entry contains several elements. Immediately after the Hebrew word stands the main gloss. The initial glosses were, in part, devised by Pleins based on his years of reading and teaching the Hebrew text. To obtain some "public domain" vocabulary, at times these words were researched in older lexicons, such as Gesenius and BDB. However, every effort has been made to avoid outmoded English words or obsolete definitions. After the initial gloss (or sometimes the gloss as such), we add alternative definitions reflecting the results of technical scholarly studies or major lexicons. These glosses will be marked by an abbreviated form of the author's name or lexicon placed in parentheses after the alternatives. The specific works we consulted for these additional meanings can be found in the bibliography. At times, these specialized studies and lexicons agree with our initial gloss, and so in many cases we are only adding further possible meanings as suggested by these works. The student may be perplexed at the wide array of proposed meanings. One of our objects is to alert the student to debates about the meanings of many words, especially those that are rare. Students will want to consult commentaries for further insight into these debates. Lastly, the entry contains a biblical verse for reference. While in some cases the choice simply provides an example of usage, many of these were selected with a view to presenting the word in a context in which the meaning is more readily apparent. The vivid nature of passages in Proverbs, for example, often makes the meaning of the Hebrew word much more memorable.

One of the unique features of this work is that the words are gathered in relatively short lists, allowing the student to build up a working vocabulary in manageable blocks. For long lists, we suggest dividing them into groups of seven for ease of memorization.[4] In fact, a general familiarity with a particular list can help jar a reader's thinking when encountering the same word in the biblical text. This is even the case when a particular word in the list has not yet been fully committed to memory. Rapid vocabulary review is likewise made easier through the shortness of the lists.

The lists are mainly alphabetized in Hebrew order. Sometimes there will be an arrangement that follows an underlying logic, as in the case of "Human Anatomy," which runs from head to toe. On rare occasions, as with "Trees," we use the English order to ease memorization. In general, if the word appears only in the plural form, we

---

4. Studies show that memorizing words in groups of up to seven is more effective. See Jeremy P. Thompson, "Word-List Size and Biblical Hebrew Vocabulary Learning," *Hebrew Higher Education* 14 (2012): 47–61.

print the plural form here. However, if a word is in a construct state or has a possessive suffix or a preposition, we remove those and provide the lexical form. Because of range of meaning and to keep some lists more complete, a few words appear in multiple lists, e.g. קִנָּמוֹן, "cinnamon," which appears in both "Herbs and Spices" and "Ointment/ Perfume." Lastly, words not appearing in the Old Testament are not included here.

We do not arrange words within lists by frequency. This is done out of a recognition that an ancient reader would have known most, if not all, of the words in a given category. To achieve such fluency, the student needs to be ready to recognize a word regardless of how "rare" it is. Lacking this level of familiarity, a student's reading of Scripture in the original language all too often becomes an act of decipherment. Inasmuch as this book does not arrange vocabulary by frequency, it is designed to complement, not replace, the books (mentioned in footnote 1) that do. Users may be interested to know, therefore, the nature of this complementarity in this connection. According to Andersen and Forbes' *Vocabulary of the Old Testament*, there are 9,980 unique words in the OT, only roughly 21 percent (2,148 words) of which occur ten times or more.[5] However, many of the words in our book occur fewer than ten times: low-frequency words.

Yet users can still gauge the relative frequency of words in our lists. As an aid to learners, we have marked all hapax legomena with an "H" and all words used less than ten times with an "R" for "rare."[6] This has two aims. First, students who wish to focus on high-frequency vocabulary within a list can do so. Second, given that the definitions of hapax legomena and rare words are more contested, the reader can be aware that the definitions of words marked "H" or "R" are more tentative. Phrases only appearing once are also marked with an "H" or an "R." Of course, not all such words are equally well understood or explained by the lexicographers, and so students should exercise caution in this regard, consulting the commentaries (or the bibliography of this volume) for the more obscure passages. Scholars will necessarily dispute some of the translations offered here, but we would suggest that for the learner it is useful to have a working definition for a word, even if one discovers through further study that a particular word's meaning is rather speculative. Thus, we have erred on the side of inclusivity in these lists, including words whose definitions might be highly contested.

Students who become familiar with the various lists in this book will find large tracts of Scripture open to them. This is the case not merely for the more popular biblical narratives but also for texts that at first blush seem more advanced. A student who tackles the worship and cultic terms gathered here, for example, will learn to

---

5. Francis I. Anderson and A. Dean Forbes, *The Vocabulary of the Old Testament* (Rome: Pontifical Biblical Institute, 1989), 8.

6. Vocabulary frequency data drawn from David J. A. Clines, ed., *The Concise Dictionary of Classical Hebrew* (Sheffield, UK: Sheffield Phoenix Press, 2009). Phrases in this book will not have "H" or "R" marked, but most of them are infrequent or *hapax*. A *hapax legomenon* ("spoken once" in Greek) is a word that only appears once in a text. The Old Testament has over 1,300 *hapax legomena*: Moisés Silva, *Biblical Words and Their Meaning: An Introduction to Lexical Semantics*, rev. and exp. ed. (Grand Rapids: Zondervan, 1995), 42; Frederick E. Greenspahn, *Hapax Legomena in Biblical Hebrew: A Study of the Phenomenon and Its Treatment since Antiquity with Special Reference to Verbal Forms* (1983; repr., Eugene, OR: Wipf and Stock, 2016).

appreciate the rhythm and poetic sensibilities of a book such as Leviticus. Too often such biblical texts remain closed worlds for students of Biblical Hebrew. It is hoped that this book will encourage the student to tackle the whole of Scripture and not merely favorite passages.

To this end, it is also recommended that students listen to the biblical text read aloud by a professional reader.[7] By treating biblical vocabulary in this immersive fashion, readers will find their reading of the Hebrew Bible to be a much more rewarding and enriching experience, stimulating the mind and nourishing the heart.

The choice in this book has been to focus on nouns over verbs. We occasionally note participle forms that are used as nouns, and we sometimes note verbs when they seem key to the semantic field as an assistance to the student. Too often "objects" are underplayed when teaching students biblical grammar. Understandably, biblical language instruction emphasizes the Hebrew verb, primarily due to its many stems and the seemingly endless numbers of weak verbs. Unfortunately, however, when elementary grammar study comes to a close, the lack of an extensive exposure to nouns quickly leads to frustration for the student reader and ends in many wasted hours leafing through the lexicon. Our philosophy is that an ancient child did not need a dictionary to learn to read Hebrew and neither should you. (Dictionaries are for reference, not for language acquisition.) This book tries to imitate something of the immersive quality of genuine language learning by gathering words that would normally occur together in a given lexical moment. A volume built on nouns can aid students in their acquisition of verbs. Certainly, because of the close tie between verbal roots and nouns in Biblical Hebrew, it is in principle possible to construct a topical book using verbs instead of nouns. But nouns, because they can be pictured, are generally the more memorable of the two. And verbal groupings tend to be less obvious because verbal associations are far more fluid than groupings of plants, spices, containers, tools, artisans, idols, and weights. We suggest that a solid command of Hebrew nouns will make the memorization of the related verbal forms much easier in the long run. Thus, it is much better to encourage students to work extensively on nouns after their basic grammar work has been completed. Another choice made in this volume is to focus on concrete nouns, rather than abstractions or qualities. Thus, though we have words for "teachers" and "students," we do not list terms for wisdom or for other abstract qualities such as fear or compassion. This includes the range of human emotions (which might be added to a future edition). Also, only in rare instances do we cite forms not appearing in the Hebrew Bible, such as from Sirach or the calendar of months (a future edition could easily delve into this territory).

How To Use *BHVCC*

These lists can be used as a springboard for many different types of activities designed to help intermediate Hebrew students learn how to use the language better. One such exercise, for instance, might capitalize on the fact that certain passages in Scrip-

---

7. The website haktuvim.co.il is a marvelous resource in this regard.

ture contain several words clustered together from one list. The teacher might ask students to examine these passages to try to determine how various items on the corresponding list relate to one another. This could be done as part of a lesson on semantics and biblical interpretation.[8] Examples of what we call "cluster verses" will be found in appendix two. These lists can also be used as sources for exploring the nuances of individual words or as exercises accompanying the presentation of information on the historical and sociolinguistic aspects of Biblical Hebrew.[9] For example, two words might have the same denotation yet vary stylistically: one poetic while the other prosaic. Alternatively, one word might be earlier and the other later in time, and students could examine passages that reveal the chronological development of words and word groups. For example, מְגִלָּה is a later term than סֵפֶר, though both refer to books or scrolls. These lists might also reveal pecularities of a particular book's style. For example, the usual biblical word for "witness" is עֵד, but Proverbs instead uses יָפִיחַ. Studying Hebrew using these lists could also reveal dialectical differences between words used in Israel and in Judah. Such exercises would give students a rich appreciation of the historical sweep of the texts brought together under one roof. Inasmuch as these lists contain so many rare words, these lists could be used as part of an exercise in figuring out the contextual meaning of infrequent words, especially hapax legomena. Even if a word will always defy easy definition, it is useful for students to know how scholars approach what sounds like a simple question: How do we know what a word means? Lastly, this book might be very useful for programs teaching Biblical Hebrew using communicative pedagogy, since these lists supply many terms used in daily life.[10]

In addition to the appendices providing bibliographies and cluster verses for each category, we have also included a master index of Hebrew words at the end of the book for the convenience of the student. In the index we do not distinguish between homonyms, words that are spelled the same but have different meanings. Readers should keep in mind the possibility that the words may indeed be true homonyms with varied histories and grammatical roots that have dovetailed in a particular form.

---

8. A good introduction to lexical semantics and biblical interpretation, though it focuses on Greek rather than Hebrew, is Moisés Silva, *Biblical Words and Their Meaning: An Introduction to Lexical Semantics*, rev. and exp. ed. (Grand Rapids: Zondervan, 1995). On Biblical Hebrew semantics, the writings of those associated with the Semantics of Ancient Hebrew Database (SAHD) and the Semantic Dictionary of Biblical Hebrew (SDBH) are useful. On SAHD, see T. Muraoka, *Studies in Ancient Hebrew Semantics*, Abr-Nahrain Supplement Series 4 (Louvain: Peeters, 1995); H. G. M. Williamson, "Semantics and Lexicography: A Methodological Conundrum," in *Biblical Lexicology: Hebrew and Greek: Semantics—Exegesis—Translation*, ed. Eberhard Bons, Jan Joosten, and Regine Hunziker-Rodewald, Beihefte zur Zeitschrift für die Alttestamentliche Wissenschaft 44 (Berlin: De Gruyter, 2015), 327–39. On SDBH, see Reinier de Blois, "Towards a New Dictionary of Biblical Hebrew Based on Semantic Domains," 2000, http://www.sdbh.org/documentation/Paper_SBL_2000.pdf; Enio R. Mueller, "The Semantics of Biblical Hebrew: Some Remarks From a Cognitive Perspective," http://www.sdbh.org/documentation/EnioRMueller_SemanticsBiblicalHebrew.pdf.
9. Joel Hoffman, *In the Beginning: A Short History of the Hebrew Language* (New York: New York University Press, 2006); William M. Schniedewind, *A Social History of Hebrew: Its Origins Through the Rabbinic Period* (New Haven: Yale University Press, 2013).
10. See, for example, Randall Buth's *Living Biblical Hebrew* and Paul Overland's *Learning Biblical Hebrew Interactively* curricula. See Paul Overland, "Can Communicative Methods Enhance Ancient Language Acquisition?," *Teaching Theology & Religion* 7, no. 1 (2004): 51–57.

Acknowledgments

Invariably, in such a compilation, there will be omissions (intended or not) and errors. In the interest of providing an accurate resource for students to build their vocabulary, the authors encourage readers to contact them regarding any additions and corrections that will help keep this book as useful as possible. The authors can be contacted at these e-mail addresses: jpleins@scu.edu and jdhomrighausen@gmail.com.

We hope that this book will open you to the promised land of a more satisfying experience of reading the Hebrew Bible. We also hope that this volume will aid in deepening your appreciation of Scripture, enliven your explorations of its wisdom, and open you at long last to the varied and vital vocabulary used by our spiritual forebearers.

Inasmuch as this work has proven to be a genuine collaboration, we would like to say a few words about the division of labor. David Pleins created the initial word lists from his research, teaching, and observation, and developed the schema of categories and subcategories. Jonathan Homrighausen consulted a number of specialized studies, and where these supplied new words or new nuances of words already on our lists, crediting the source in parentheses. (Appendix one indicates which ones were more useful to encourage further study of the rich resources available.) He also created the appendices and checked every word in the book against David Clines' Dictionary of Classical Hebrew, both to consult its definition and to mark words as either infrequent or hapax. Both authors contributed to this preface. Any oversights, of course, remain our own.

We are grateful to Dr. Nancy Erickson, Senior Editor of Biblical Languages, Textbooks, and Reference at Zondervan Academic, for her enthusiastic support of this book from the moment it crossed the transom. Jonathan Homrighausen would like to thank Rabbi Larry Moldo and Andrea Moldo, Catherine Murphy, Barbara Green, and David Pleins, who took the time to teach him Hebrew. In addition to his wife and mother, to whom he dedicates this book, he would like to thank his new family: Kate, Dave, Matt, Kelley, Laura, Pat, and Chet, who have taken him in as one of their own and never once complained when he brought work for this book to family gatherings. Because of this fruitful collaboration, David Pleins wishes to express his debt to and admiration of Jonathan Homrighausen, a graduate student and research assistant of unparalleled creativity, insight, and dedication to this project. He is grateful as well to his teachers and early mentors in Biblical Hebrew: Belinda Bicknell and Dr. Charles Krahmalkov, who valued exactitude over cleverness. He also wishes to express gratitude to Karen for her computer, her humor, her wisdom, and her love of life.

BIBLIOGRAPHY

Aitken, J. K. *The Semantics of Blessing and Cursing in Ancient Hebrew*. Ancient Near Eastern Studies Supplement 23. Louvain: Peeters, 2007.

———. "מַעֲגָל." In *Semantics of Ancient Hebrew*, edited by T. Muraoka, 79–85. Abr-Nahrain Supplement Series 6. Louvain: Peeters, 1998.

———. "מִשְׁעוֹל." In *Semantics of Ancient Hebrew*, edited by T. Muraoka, 86–88. Abr-Nahrain Supplement Series 6. Louvain: Peeters, 1998.

———. "נָקַב II." In *Semantics of Ancient Hebrew*, edited by T. Muraoka, 101–5. Abr-Nahrain Supplement Series 6. Louvain: Peeters, 1998.

Amzallag, Nissim. "Copper Metallurgy: A Hidden Fundament of the Theology of Ancient Israel?" *Scandinavian Journal of the Old Testament* 27, no. 2 (2013): 151–69.

———. "Furnace Remelting as the Expression of YHWH's Holiness: Evidence from the Meaning of Qannâ in the Divine Context." *Journal of Biblical Literature* 134, no. 2 (2015): 233–52.

Barr, James. *Biblical Words for Time*. Naperville, IL: A. R. Allenson, 1962.

Boer, Roland. "The Patriarch's Nuts: Concerning the Testicular Logic of Biblical Hebrew." *Journal of Men, Masculinities & Spirituality* 5, no. 2 (2011): 41–52.

Borowski, Oded. *Agriculture in Iron Age Israel*. Winona Lake, IN: Eisenbrauns, 1987.

———. *Daily Life in Biblical Times*. Archaeology and Biblical Studies 5. Atlanta: Society of Biblical Literature, 2003.

———. *Every Living Thing: Daily Use of Animals in Ancient Israel*. Walnut Creek, CA: AltaMira Press, 1999.

Bovati, Pietro. *Re-Establishing Justice: Legal Terms, Concepts and Procedures in the Hebrew Bible*. Translated by Michael J. Smith. Journal for the Study of the Old Testament Supplement Series 105. Sheffield, UK: Sheffield Academic Press, 1994.

Braun, Joachim. *Music in Ancient Israel/Palestine: Archaeological, Written and Comparative Sources*. Translated by Douglas W. Stott. Grand Rapids: Eerdmans, 2002.

Brenner, Athalya. *Colour Terms in the Old Testament*. Journal for the Study of the Old Testament Supplement Series 21. Sheffield, UK: Sheffield Academic Press, 1982.

———. "The Food of Love: Gendered Food and Food Imagery in the Song of Songs." *Semeia* 86 (1999): 101–12.

Bridge, Edward J. "The Metaphoric Use of Slave Terms in the Hebrew Bible." *Bulletin for Biblical Research* 23, no. 1 (2013): 13–28.

Burgh, Theodore W. *Listening to the Artifacts: Music Culture in Ancient Palestine*. New York: T&T Clark, 2006.

Clines, David J. A, ed. *The Dictionary of Classical Hebrew*. Sheffield: Sheffield Phoenix Press, 1993–2011.

Clines, David J. A. "Misapprehensions, Ancient and Modern, about Lions (Nahum 2.13)." Accessed May 31, 2016. https://www.academia.edu/7385702/ Misapprehensions_Ancient_and_Modern_about_Lions_Nahum_2.13_.

De Moore, Johannes, ed. כלי *Database: Utensils in the Hebrew Bible.* Het Oudtestamentisch Werkgezelschap, 2010–2016. http://www.otw-site.eu/KLY/kly.php.

Eichler, Raanan. "The Meaning of Pa'am in the Context of Furniture." *Journal of Semitic Studies* 60, no. 1 (2015): 1–18.

———. "The Meaning of Zēr." *Vetus Testamentum* 64, no. 2 (2014): 196–210.

Eng, Milton. *The Days of Our Years: A Lexical Semantic Study of the Life Cycle in Biblical Israel.* The Library of Hebrew Bible/Old Testament Studies 464. New York: Bloomsbury T&T Clark, 2011.

Grzybowski, Andrzej, and Malgorzata Nita. "Leprosy in the Bible." *Clinics in Dermatology* 34 (2016): 3–7.

Guillaume, A. "Metallurgy in the Old Testament." *Palestine Exploration Quarterly* 94, no. 2 (December 1, 1962): 129–32.

Harrison, Roland K. *Healing Herbs of the Bible.* Leiden: Brill, 1966.

Hartley, John E. *The Semantics of Ancient Hebrew Colour Lexemes.* Ancient Near Eastern Studies Supplement 33. Louvain: Peeters, 2011.

Holladay, William L., ed. *A Concise Hebrew and Aramaic Lexicon of the Old Testament.* Grand Rapids: Eerdmans, 1972.

Hobbins, John. "The Human Anatomy in Ancient Hebrew: Advanced Level." *Ancient Hebrew Poetry*, November 26, 2007. http://ancienthebrewpoetry.typepad. com/ancient_hebrew_poetry/2007/11/the-human-ana–2.html.

Hobbs, T. R. *A Time for War: A Study of Warfare in the Old Testament.* Old Testament Studies 3. Wilmington, DE: Michael Glazier, 1989.

Hope, Edward R. *All Creatures Great and Small: Living Things in the Bible.* Helps for Translators. New York: United Bible Societies, 2003.

Hurvitz, Avi. *A Concise Lexicon of Late Biblical Hebrew: Linguistic Innovations in the Writings of the Second Temple Period.* Vetus Testamentum Supplements 160. Leiden: Brill, 2014.

Jordan, David John. "An Offering of Wine: An Introductory Exploration of the Role of Wine in the Hebrew Bible and Ancient Judaism Through the Examination of the Semantics of Some Keywords." PhD diss., University of Sydney, 2002. https://ses.library.usyd.edu.au/handle/2123/482.

Kelso, James L., and W. F. Albright. "The Ceramic Vocabulary of the Old Testament." *Bulletin of the American Schools of Oriental Research Supplementary Studies*, no. 5/6 (1948): 1–48.

Koller, Aaron J. *The Semantic Field of Cutting Tools in Biblical Hebrew: The Interface of Philological, Semantic, and Archaeological Evidence.* Catholic Biblical Quarterly Monograph Series 49. Washington, DC: Catholic Biblical Association of America, 2012.

Kolyada, Yelena. *A Compendium of Musical Instruments and Instrumental Terminology in the Bible.* BibleWorld. London: Routledge, 2014.

Koops, Robert, and Donald Slager. *Each According to Its Kind: Plants and Trees in the Bible*. Helps for Translators. New York: United Bible Societies, 2012.

Kottek, Samuel S. "Hygiene and Health Care in the Bible." In *Health and Disease in the Holy Land: Studies in the History and Sociology of Medicine from Ancient Times to the Present*, edited by Manfred Waserman and Samuel S. Kottek, 37–66. Lewiston, NY: Edwin Mellen, 1996.

MacDonald, Nathan. *What Did the Ancient Israelites Eat? Diet in Biblical Times*. Grand Rapids: Eerdmans, 2008.

Massey-Gillespie, Kevin. "A New Approach to Basic Hebrew Colour Terms." *Journal of Northwest Semitic Languages* 20, no. 1 (1994): 1–11.

Miano, David. *Shadow on the Steps: Time Measurement in Ancient Israel*. Resources for Biblical Study. Atlanta: Society of Biblical Literature, 2010.

Mitchell, T. C. "The Music of the Old Testament Reconsidered." *Palestine Exploration Quarterly* 124, no. 2 (1992): 124–43.

Montagu, Jeremy. *Musical Instruments of the Bible*. Lanham, MD: Scarecrow Press, 2002.

Muraoka, T., ed. *Semantics of Ancient Hebrew*. Abr-Nahrain Supplement Series 6. Louvain: Peeters, 1998.

Nielsen, Kjeld. *Incense in Ancient Israel*. Vetus Testamentum Supplements 38. Leiden: Brill, 1986.

Noonan, Benjamin J. "There and Back Again: 'Tin' or 'Lead' in Amos 7:7–9?" *Vetus Testamentum* 63, no. 2 (2013): 299–307.

———. "Zion's Foundation: The Meaning of בֹּחַן in Isaiah 28,16." *Zeitschrift für die Alttestamentliche Wissenschaft* 125, no. 2 (2013): 314–19.

Notebaart, Cor. "Metallurgical Metaphors in the Hebrew Bible." PhD diss., Protestant Theological University, 2010.

Olyan, Saul M. *Disability in the Hebrew Bible: Interpreting Mental and Physical Differences*. Cambridge: Cambridge University Press, 2008.

Parker, Julie Faith. *Valuable and Vulnerable: Children in the Hebrew Bible, Especially the Elisha Cycle*. Brown Judaic Studies 355. Providence, RI: Brown University Press, 2013.

Patai, Raphael. *The Children of Noah: Jewish Seafaring in Ancient Times*. Princeton, NJ: Princeton University Press, 1999.

Peters, Kurtis. *Hebrew Lexical Semantics and Daily Life in Ancient Israel: What's Cooking in Biblical Hebrew?* Biblical Interpretation Series 146. Leiden: Brill, 2016.

Platt, Elizabeth. "Jewelry of Bible Times and the Catalog of Isaiah 3:18–23: Part I." *Andrews University Seminary Studies* 17, no. 1 (1979): 71–84.

———. "Jewelry of Bible Times and the Catalog of Isaiah 3:18–23: Part II." *Andrews University Seminary Studies* 17, no. 2 (1979): 189–201.

Pritz, Ray. *The Works of Their Hands: Man-Made Things in the Bible*. Helps for Translators. New York: United Bible Societies, 2009.

Rattray, S. "Marriage Rules, Kinship Terms and Family Structure in the Bible." In *1987 Seminar Papers: One Hundred Twenty-Third Annual Meeting, December 5–8, 1987*, edited by Kent Harold Richards. Atlanta: Scholars Press, 1987.

Rollston, Christopher A. *Writing and Literacy in the World of Ancient Israel: Epigraphic Evidence from the Iron Age*. Archaeology and Biblical Studies 11. Atlanta: Society of Biblical Literature, 2010.

Salvesen, Alison. "Esther 1:11; 2:17; 6:8: 'Something to Do with a Camel'?" *Journal of Semitic Studies* 44, no. 1 (1999): 35–46.

———. "The Trappings of Royalty in Ancient Hebrew." In *King and Messiah in Israel and the Ancient Near East: Proceedings of the Oxford Old Testament Seminar*, edited by John Day, 119–40. Journal for the Study of the Old Testament Supplement Series 270. Sheffield: Sheffield Academic Press, 1998.

———. "הֲדַם." In *Semantics of Ancient Hebrew*, edited by T. Muraoka, 38–43. Abr-Nahrain Supplement Series 6. Louvain: Peeters, 1998.

———. "עֲטָרָה." In *Semantics of Ancient Hebrew*, edited by T. Muraoka, 106–13. Abr-Nahrain Supplement Series 6. Louvain: Peeters, 1998.

———. "שֵׁבֶט." In *Semantics of Ancient Hebrew*, edited by T. Muraoka, 122–36. Abr-Nahrain Supplement Series 6. Louvain: Peeters, 1998.

Scott, R. B. Y. "Meteorological Phenomena and Terminology in the Old Testament." *Zeitschrift Für Die Alttestamentliche Wissenschaft* 64, no. 1 (1952): 11–25.

———. "Weights and Measures of the Bible." *The Biblical Archaeologist* 22, no. 2 (1959): 22–40.

Seevers, Boyd. *Warfare in the Old Testament: The Organization, Weapons, and Tactics of Ancient Near Eastern Armies*. Grand Rapids: Kregel Academic, 2013.

Shafer-Elliott, Cynthia. "Food in the Hebrew Bible." *Biblical Interpretation*, May 2013. http://www.bibleinterp.com/articles/2013/sha378013.shtml.

———. *Food in Ancient Judah: Domestic Cooking in the Time of the Hebrew Bible*. BibleWorld. Sheffield, UK: Routledge, 2013.

Sherwin, Simon J. "In Search of Trees: Isaiah XLIV 14 and Its Implications." *Vetus Testamentum* 53, no. 4 (2003): 514–29.

Smith, John Arthur. *Music in Ancient Judaism and Early Christianity*. Burlington, VT: Ashgate Publishing, 2011.

Stadelmann, Luis I. J. *The Hebrew Conception of the World: A Philological and Literary Study*. Analecta Biblica 39. Rome: Pontifical Biblical Institute, 1970.

Steiner, Richard C. *Stockmen from Tekoa, Sycomores from Sheba: A Study of Amos' Occupations*. Catholic Biblical Quarterly Monograph Series 36. Washington, DC: Catholic Biblical Association, 2003.

Stewart, David Tabb. "Sexual Disabilities in the Hebrew Bible." In *Disability Studies and Biblical Literature*, edited by Candida Moss and Jeremy Schipper, 67–88. New York: Palgrave Macmillan, 2011.

Stieglitz, Robert R. "Hebrew Seafaring in the Biblical Period." In *Seafaring and the Jews*, edited by Nadav Kashtan, 5–15. London: Frank Cass, 2001.

Toorn, Karel Van der. *Scribal Culture and the Making of the Hebrew Bible*. Cambridge, MA: Harvard University Press, 2009.

United Bible Societies. *Semantic Dictionary of Biblical Hebrew*. 2000–2009. http://www.sdbh.org/dictionary/main.php?language=en.

United Bible Societies. *Fauna and Flora of the Bible*. Helps for Translators. London: United Bible Societies, 1980.

Walsh, Carey. *The Fruit of the Vine: Viticulture in Ancient Israel*. Harvard Semitic Monographs 60. Winona Lake, IN: Eisenbrauns, 2000.

Way, Kenneth C. "Donkey Domain: Zechariah 9:9 and Lexical Semantics." *Journal of Biblical Literature* 129, no. 1 (2010): 105–14.

Widder, Wendy. *"To Teach" in Ancient Israel: A Cognitive Linguistic Study of a Biblical Hebrew Lexical Set*. Beihefte Zur Zeitschrift Für Die Alttestamentliche Wissenschaft 456. Boston: De Gruyter, 2014.

Wiggins, Steve A. *Weathering the Psalms: A Meteorotheological Survey*. Eugene, OR: Cascade Books, 2014.

Wilkinson, John. "The Body in the Old Testament." *Evangelical Quarterly* 63 (1991): 195–210.

Williams, Gillian Patricia. "A Talmudic Perspective on Old Testament Diseases, Physicians and Remedies." MA thesis, University of South Africa, 2009. http://uir.unisa.ac.za/handle/10500/3318.

Zatelli, Ida. "Astrology and the Worship of the Stars in the Bible." *Zeitschrift Für Die Alttestamentliche Wissenschaft* 103, no. 1 (2009): 86–99.

Zhakevich, Philip. "The Tools of an Israelite Scribe: A Semantic Study of the Terms Signifying the Tools and Materials of Writing in Biblical Hebrew." PhD diss., University of Texas, Austin, 2015. https://repositories.lib.utexas.edu/handle/2152/31558.

PART I

THE CREATED ORDER

HEAVENS AND EARTH

Cosmology

אַרְבַּע כַּנְפוֹת הָאָרֶץ four corners of the earth (HCW) (Isa 11:12)

טַבּוּר הָאָרֶץ navel, center of the earth = Jerusalem (HCW) (Ezek 38:12)

יַרְכְּתֵי־אָרֶץ remote parts of the earth (HCW) (Jer 6:22)

הַכֹּל the universe (HCW) (Ps 119:91)

עוֹלָם world, creation, created order (DCH) (Eccl 3:11)

קַצְוֵי־אָרֶץ ends of the earth, boundaries of the firmament (HCW) (Ps 48:11)

Sky/Firmament

אֲגֻדָּה vault (holding up the sky) (Amos 9:6 R)

אֲרֻבֹּת הַשָּׁמַיִם "the windows of heaven," holes in the firmament through which rain comes (HCW) (Gen 7:11)

דְּלָתַיִם doors of the firmament, through which rain comes (HCW) (Job 38:8)

חוּג הָאָרֶץ horizon; boundary between earth and heaven (HCW) (Isa 40:22)

חוּג שָׁמַיִם horizon; boundary between earth and heaven (HCW); firmament (SDBH) (Job 22:14)

מַבּוּל waters above the firmament (HCW) (Gen 6:17)

עֲרִיפִים skies, clouds, mists (Isa 5:30 H)

רָקִיעַ sky-dome, firmament (Ezek 1:22–23)

שָׁמַיִם sky, heaven (Gen 7:9)

Stars

אוֹר luminary (Gen 1:3)

הֵילֵל the morning-star (Venus) (Isa 14:12 H)

כּוֹכָב star (Job 25:5)

כִּיּוּן Saturn (HCW) (Amos 5:26 H)

כִּימָה Pleiades, cluster of stars (Amos 5:8 R)

כְּסִיל Orion, constellation (Job 9:9 R)

מַזָּלוֹת planets, Zodiac signs ("inn" of sun); Mazzaroth, a star or constellation (DCH) (2 Kgs 23:5 H)

מַזָּרוֹת twelve stations of the sun during its yearly orbit (Zatelli); Mazzaroth, a star or constellation (DCH) (Job 38:32 H)

עֵז she-goat; goat hair, the She-goat (constellation) (DCH) (Amos 5:9)

עַיִשׁ/עָשׁ Great Bear (Ursa Major); Aldebaran or Arcturus, the Great Bear (Job 38:32 H)

שׁוֹר Taurus (in Zodiac) (DCH); single head of cattle, bullock; ox (ELT) (Amos 5:9)

Sun

חַמָּה sun, heat (Ps 19:7 R)
חֲרָבוֹן dryness, heat of summer (Wiggins) (Ps 32:4 H)
חֶרֶס sun (SDBH) (Judg 14:18 R)
צַח sunny, bright (Isa 18:4 R)
שֶׁמֶשׁ sun (Gen 15:12)

Moon

חֹדֶשׁ new moon (HCW) (Num 10:10)
יָרֵחַ moon (Josh 10:12–13)
כֶּסֶא full moon (Prov 7:20 R)
לְבָנָה moon; white (Song 6:10 R)

Earth

General

אִי island (Isa 23:2)
אֶרֶץ earth, land; dry native clay (Kelso and Albright) (Ps 12:7)
חֶבֶל הַיָּם coastal plain (HCW) (Zeph 2:5–6)
חֶדֶל era, age, lifetime, space of the world (HCW) (Isa 38:11 R)
חֶלֶד world, duration (Ps 17:14)
חוֹחַ hole, crevice (SDBH) (1 Sam 13:6 H)
יַבָּשָׁה dry land (Gen 1:9)
יְשִׁימוֹן wilderness; Jeshimon (SDBH) (Num 21:20)
מִמְכָּר mortgaged land, land sold; merchandise; ancestral land (DCH) (Deut 18:8 R)
מַעֲנָה furrow (SDBH) (1 Sam 14:14 R)
מַשְׁקֶה well-irrigated land (HCW) (Gen 13:10 R)
עָקֹב steep ground (HCW) (Isa 40:4 H)
שָׁרָב hot ground reflecting mirage (MPTOT); parched ground (DCH) (Isa 35:7 R)
שָׂדֶה field (Stadelmann); countryside, bush, uninhabited land (SDBH) (Gen 2:5)
תֵּבֵל earth, globe, land (1 Sam 2:8)
תֵּל tell, mound (HCW) (Josh 8:28 R)

Soil

אָבָק dusty soil, stirred up by wind (HCW) (Exod 9:9 R)
אֲדָמָה land, soil (Gen 2:5); topsoil, humus (HCW); dry native clay (Kelso and Albright) (Isa 45:9)
בֹּץ wet mire near bodies of water (Zhakevich) (Jer 38:22 H)
דַּכָּא dust (SDBH) (Ps 90:3)
חוֹל sand (HCW) (Gen 32:13)
חֹמֶר clay (HCW); worked clay (Kelso and Albright); mud, clay, mortar (SDBH) (Isa 10:6)

טִיט mud, mire, silt, clay (HCW) (Job 41:22)

יָוֵן mud, mire (Zhakevich) (Ps 40:3 R)

מְעָה grain of sand (SDBH) (Isa 48:19 H)

נִיר untilled soil (Jer 4:3 R)

עָפָר dust, raw clay (Kelso and Albright) (Job 10:9)

רֶגֶב clod of earth (SDBH) (Job 21:33 R)

רֶפֶשׁ mud, mire, foam (Zhakevich) (Isa 57:20 H)

Mountain
General

הַר mountain, range (Gen 22:2)

הָרָר mountain (Deut 33:15)

מַדְרֵגָה mountain escarpment, cliff (HCW) (Ezek 38:20 R)

מַעֲלֶה pass between mountains or hills (HCW) (Josh 15:7)

Top/Rock/Height

אָמִיר summit; branch (of tree) DCH) (Isa 17:6 R)

רֹאשׁ top of mountain (HCW) (Gen 8:5)

רֶכֶס mountain ridge, rugged place (Isa 40:4 H)

שֵׁן peak of mountain (HCW); tooth, crag of rock (DCH) (Job 39:28)

שְׁפִי bare mountain, height (Num 23:3)

Slope/Terrace/Ridge

אָשֵׁד slope (Josh 10:40 R)

אֲשֵׁדֹת slopes of a mountain (HCW) (Deut 3:17 R)

גַּבְנֻנִּים peaks, ridges of a mountain (HCW) (Ps 68:16 R)

גְּדוּד ridge; barrier, wall (SDBH) (2 Sam 22:30 R)

כָּתֵף slope of mountain (HCW) (Num 34:11)

מוֹרָד slope of mountain (HCW) (Josh 7:5 R)

צֵלָע terrace cut in the side of a mountain (HCW); side, mountain slope (DCH) (2 Sam 16:13)

Foot/Base

מוֹסְדֵי הָרִים foundations of mountains (HCW) (Deut 32:22 H)

תַּחְתִּית foot of a mountain (HCW) (Exod 19:17)

Hill

גִּבְעָה hillock (Isa 40:4)

נֶפֶת hill (?) (SDBH); height, hill-country (DCH) (Josh 17:11 R)

קֶרֶן hill (SDBH) (Isa 5:1 H)

רְכָסִים hillocks (HCW); rough place, uneven ground (DCH) (Isa 40:4 H)

שְׁפִי bare hill, plain (Isa 49:9)

Valley

בִּקְעָה	valley (Amos 1:5)
גַּיְא	valley (HCW) (Isa 22:1)
כִּכָּר	valley, circle; district (DCH) (Gen 13:10)
מִישׁוֹר	plain, plateau (HCW) (Isa 40:4)
עֵמֶק	valley, lowland (1 Chr 12:16)
שְׁפֵלָה	lowland (HCW) (Deut 1:7)

Desert/Steppe

חָרְבָּה	desolation, desert (HCW) (Isa 44:26)
חֲרֵרִים	dry places, parched places (SDBH) (Jer 17:6 H)
יְשִׁימוֹן	desert waste (Ps 107:4)
מִדְבָּר	desert, wilderness, pasture; also steppe (HCW) (Gen 4:20)
מְלֵחָה	saltness, barrenness, salt flat (HCW) (Job 39:6 R)
נָוֶה	steppe (HCW) (Jer 9:9)
עֲרָבָה	desert plain, steppe (Deut 1:1)
צִיָּה	dryness, desert land (HCW) (Isa 35:1)
צָיוֹן	dryness, parched ground (HCW) (Isa 25:5 R)
צִמָּאוֹן	thirsty ground (HCW) (Isa 35:7 R)
שַׁמָּה	devastation, waste (HCW) (Jer 51:43)

Cave

מְעָרָה	cave (Gen 19:3)

Rock/Stone/Pebble

אֶבֶן	stone (Gen 35:14)
חַלָּמִישׁ	flint (HCW) (Deut 8:15 R)
חָצָץ	gravel (HCW) (Prov 20:17 R)
כֵּף	rock (Jer 4:29 R)
אֶבֶן מַעֲמָסָה	heavy stone (SDBH); stone of burden (DCH) (Zech 12:3)
מַסָּע	quarry; missile, dart (1 Kgs 6:7 R)
מַקֶּבֶת	quarry (SDBH) (Isa 51:1 H)
סֶלַע	rock, crag, cliff (Amos 6:12)
פּוּר	small pebble or potsherd used to make decisions = lot (SDBH) (Esth 3:7 R)
צוּר	rock (Deut 8:15)
צַר / צֹר	flint (HCW) (Isa 5:28 R)
צְרוֹר	pebble (HCW); tiny grain (SDBH) (2 Sam 17:13 R)
שְׁבָרִים	stone quarries (SDBH); Shebarim (DCH) (Josh 7:5 H)

Clouds

חָזִיז	raincloud, thundercloud (MPTOT); thunderstorm (DCH) (Zech 10:1 R)

נָשִׂיא   clouds, mist, vapor; ruler (Jer 10:13 R)

עָב   dark cloud; rain cloud, thundercloud (MPTOT); cumulus clouds (Wiggins) (Judg 5:4)

עָנָן   cloud, fog, mist, morning fog (MPTOT); "pillar of cloud" (Ps 78:14)

עֲנַן בֹּקֶר   morning fog (MPTOT) (Hos 6:4)

עֲנָנָה   cloud, cloudy (Job 3:5 H)

עֲרָפֶל   dark threatening cloud, thundercloud (MPTOT) (1 Kgs 8:12)

קִיטוֹר   dense cloud (MPTOT); smoke (DCH) (Ps 148:8 R)

שַׁחַק   dust, cloud; cirrus clouds (Wiggins) (Ps 89:7)

Wind/Hurricane

גַּלְגַּל / גִּלְגָּל   whirlwind; wheel (Ps 77:19)

מְזָרִים   north winds, scatterers (Job 37:9)

סוּפָה   hurricane, storm-wind (Job 37:9)

סַעַר / שַׂעַר / סְעָרָה   hurricane, tempest; wind-storm, gale (MPTOT) (Ps 55:9 R)

רוּחַ   wind; spirit (Ps 1:4)

רוּחַ מִדְבָּר   desert wind (HCW) (Jer 13:24)

Lightning

אֵשׁ   fire, lightning (Wiggins) (Ps 11:6)

בָּזָק   flash of lightning (Ezek 1:14 H)

בָּרָק   lightning; flashing sword (Ps 18:15)

גַּחֶלֶת   coal of fire, (metaphorically) lightning (Wiggins) (Isa 47:14)

חָזִיז   flash of lightning (Job 28:26 R)

חֲנָמָל   lightning (Wiggins); frost, flood (DCH) (Ps 78:47 H)

רַעַם   thunder (Wiggins) (Ps 77:19 R)

רֶשֶׁף   flames, (metaphorically) lightning (Wiggins) (Ps 78:48)

Fire

אוּר   fire, eastern country (SDBH) (Isa 31:9 R)

אֵפֶר   ashes (SDBH) (Gen 18:27)

אֵשׁ   fire (SDBH) (Gen 15:17)

יָקוּד   hearth (CHB); glowing fire (כְּלִי) (Isa 30:14 H)

כִּידוֹד   spark of flame (SDBH) (Job 41:11 H)

לַהַב   flame (SDBH) (Judg 13:20)

מוֹקֵד   fire, burning (of God's judgment) (SDBH) (Isa 33:14 R)

נִיצוֹץ   spark (SDBH) (Isa 1:31 H)

שְׂרֵפָה   burning, fire, incineration, funeral pyre (Gen 11:3)

Rain/Storm

General

בַּצֹּרֶת   drought (DCH) (Jer 14:1 R)

גֶּשֶׁם/גֹּשֶׁם   shower, rain; winter rain (Wiggins) (1 Kgs 18:45)

הַוּוֹת   storm (?) (Wiggins); wind, bluster, boast (DCH) (Ps 57:2)

זַרְזִיף   pouring rain (Ps 72:6 H)

זֶרֶם   thunderstorm, gush of water, storm; rain-storm, downpour (HCW) (Isa 4:6 R)

מָטַר/מָטָר   rain (Deut 11:11)

מַיִם   waters, rain (Wiggins) (Ps 77:18)

נֶפֶץ   driving storm; cloudburst (DCH) (Isa 30:30 H)

סַגְרִיר   steady, pouring rain (Prov 27:15 H)

קֶשֶׁת   rainbow (Gen 9:13)

רְבִיבִים   heavy rains; showers (DCH); spring rains (MPTOT) (Deut 32:2 R)

שָׂעִיר   a shower, small rain (Deut 32:2 H)

שַׂעַר   tempest; terror (Isa 28:2 R)

שׁוֹאָה/שׁוֹא   tempest; ruin; sudden destructive storm (MPTOT) (Ps 35:8)

Spring Rain

מַלְקוֹשׁ   spring rain (later) (Deut 11:14 R)

רְבִיבִים   heavy rains; showers (DCH); spring rains (MPTOT) (Deut 32:2 R)

Autumn Rain

יוֹרֶה   autumn rain (early) (Deut 11:14 R)

מוֹרֶה   autumn rain (MPTOT) (Joel 2:23 R)

Hail

אֶבֶן   hailstone (SDBH) (Josh 10:11)

אֶלְגָּבִישׁ   hail; hailstone (SDBH) (Ezek 13:11 R)

בָּרָד   hail (MPTOT) (Ezra 10:9)

Water

General

בְּאֵר   well, watering place, spring (SDBH) (Gen 16:14); tar pit, bitumen pit (Gen 14:10)

בּוֹר   pit; cistern (Gen 37:20) (SDBH)

בְּרֵכָה   pool (2 Sam 2:13) (SDBH)

גֵּב/גֶּבֶא   pool, puddle (SDBH); trench, cistern (DCH) (2 Kgs 3:16 R)

מַיִם   water (Gen 21:14)

מִפְרָץ   bay (HCW); wadi (DCH) (Judg 5:17 H)

Swamp

אֲגַם   swamp, marsh, reedy pool (HCW); pool, swamp (DCH) (Exod 7:19 R)

בִּצָּה   swamp, marsh (SDBH) (Job 8:11 R)

Sea/Ocean

אֲפִקֵי יָם   channels on the bottom of the sea (HCW) (2 Sam 22:16 R)

גַּל   wave of sea (HCW) (Isa 48:18)

חֵקֶר תְּהוֹם   recesses of the deep (poetic for "depths of sea") (HCW) (Job 38:16)

יָם   sea; west (Gen 49:13)

מִבְּכִי נְהָרוֹת   sources of the rivers (HCW) (Job 28:11)

מַעֲמַקֵּי־יָם   depths of the sea (HCW) (Isa 51:10)

מְצֻלוֹת יָם   depths of the sea (HCW) (Mic 7:19)

מִשְׁבָּר   wave breaking against shore (HCW) (Ps 93:4 R)

נִבְכֵי־יָם   springs of the sea (poetic) (HCW) (Job 38:16)

קַרְקַע הַיָּם   sea-bed; floor; bottom of the sea (HCW) (Amos 9:3)

תְּהוֹם   abyss, deep; ocean, great deep (SDBH) (Amos 7:4)

Dew

אֶגְלֵי־טָל   drops of dew (HCW) (Job 38:28 H)

טַל   dew, mist (Ps 110:3)

רְסִיסֵי לָיְלָה   nighttime dew (HCW) (Song 5:2)

Spring/Source

בְּאֵר / בְּיר   tar pit, bitumen pit; well, watering place, spring (SDBH) (Gen 16:14)

גֻּלָּה   spring (SDBH) (Josh 15:19)

מַבּוּעַ   fountain, spring (Isa 35:7 R)

מַעְיָן   fountain, source (Isa 41:18)

מָקוֹר   spring, source, well (Jer 2:13)

נֵבֶךְ   fountain, spring (Job 38:16 H)

עַיִן   spring; eye (Exod 15:27)

Flood

יְבוּל / יָבָל   flood (HCW) (Job 20:28)

מַבּוּל   flood; the Flood; deluge, frost, sleet (SDBH) (Ps 29:10)

נֹזְלִים   floods, streams (HCW) (Exod 15:8)

שֶׁטֶף   flood, downpour (Nah 1:8 R)

שׁוֹט   outburst of water (DCH) (Isa 28:15 R)

River/Stream

אַרְבָּעָה רָאשִׁים   four branch streams, head streams (HCW) (Gen 2:10)

גִּדְיָה/גְּדָה riverbank (Isa 8:7 R)

יְאֹר channel (Job 28:10), the Nile (Gen 41:1), later the Tigris (Dan 12:5–7) (HCW); stream (SDBH)

יוּבַל/אוּבַל/יָבָל stream, watercourse (Isa 30:25 R)

מִיכָל little stream (2 Sam 17:20 H)

נָהָר river, stream (Isa 44:27); the Euphrates (HCW) (Gen 31:21)

פֶּלֶג/פְּלָגוֹת river, stream; water channel (HCW) (Isa 30:25 R)

שִׁבֹּלֶת flowing stream, flood (HCW) (Isa 27:12 R)

Valley/Ravine

אָפִיק ravine, stream, tube; wadi, watercourse (SDBH) (Job 6:15)

אֲשֵׁדָה ravine, slope (Josh 12:8 R)

בַּתָּה ravine (SDBH) (Isa 7:19 H)

גַּיְא gorge, valley (Isa 40:4)

נַחַל wadi, stream, valley, torrent (Gen 26:19)

עָרוּץ holes in ground caused by erosion of gullies (HCW) (Job 30:6 H)

שׁוּחָה gorge, pits; pit (SDBH); pit, ravine (DCH) (Prov 22:14 R)

Channel/Canal

אוּבָל canal (SDBH) (Dan 8:2 R)

יְאֹר channel, canal, Nile (Exod 7:19)

פֶּלֶג/פְּלָגוֹת river, stream; water-channel (HCW) (Isa 30:25 R)

שֶׁלַח water-conduit (man-made) (SDBH) (Neh 3:15 R)

תְּעָלָה channel, watercourse; bandage (Job 38:25 R)

Cold/Ice

כְּפוֹר hoar-frost (Job 38:29 R)

קָרָה cold (Ps 147:17 R)

קֶרַח ice; frost (DCH) (Gen 31:40 R)

שֶׁלֶג/שָׁלֶג snow (Ps 51:9)

Underworld

אֶרֶץ תַּחְתִּיּוֹת/ אֶרֶץ תַּחְתִּית/ אֶרֶץ תַּחְתִּיוֹת land of the lowest parts, underworld (HCW) (Ezek 26:20)

אֲבַדּוֹן place of destruction, underworld (HCW); Abaddon, world of the dead (SDBH) (Ps 88:12 R)

בּוֹר pit, underworld (poetic) (HCW) (Ezek 31:14)

בּוֹר שָׁאוֹן pit of Destruction (HCW) (Ps 40:3)

בּוֹר תַּחְתִּיּוֹת pit of the lowest part, underworld (poetic) (HCW) (Lam 3:55)

יַרְכְּתֵי־בוֹר recesses of the pit, underworld (poetic) (HCW) (Isa 14:15)

עָפָר dust, underworld (poetic) (HCW) (Ps 22:30)

קֶבֶר grave, world of the dead (SDBH) (Ps 88:12)

שְׁאוֹל Sheol, realm of the dead (HCW) (Gen 37:35)

שַׁחַת pit, pitfall, netherworld (Isa 38:17)

Compass/Directions

North

צָפוֹן north; north wind (HCW) (Song 4:16)

שְׂמֹאל left side, north (HCW) (Gen 14:15)

צָפֹנָה northward (DCH) (Num 2:25 R)

South

דָּרוֹם south, south-wind (Deut 33:23)

נֶגֶב south (Exod 26:18)

תֵּימָן south; south wind (HCW, SDBH) (Ps 78:26)

תֵּימָנָה southward (HCW) (Exod 26:18 R)

East

אוּר eastern country; fire (SDBH) (Isa 24:15 R)

מוֹצָא place of sunrise, east (HCW) (Ps 75:7)

מִזְרָח east, place of sunrise (HCW) (Josh 4:19)

קָדִים east; East-wind, Scirocco (MPTOT) (Ps 48:8)

קֶדֶם east (Gen 25:6)

קַדְמוֹנִי eastern (Ezek 11:1)

West

אָחוֹר west; behind (2 Sam 1:22)

יָם west; sea (Deut 11:24)

מָבוֹא west, sunset (Deut 11:30)

מַעֲרָב place of sunset, the west (HCW) (Ps 75:7)

METALS, STONES, GEMS, MINERALS, AND PEARLS
Metals

Gold

בֶּצֶר   precious ore (Guillame); gold (DCH, Notebaart) (Job 22:25 R)

זָהָב   gold (Gen 2:11)

טָהוֹר זָהָב   pure or purified gold (cultic context) (Notebaart) (Exod 25:11)

מְזֻקָּק זָהָב   washed gold (Notebaart); refined, purified gold (DCH) (1 Chr 28:18)

סָגוּר זָהָב   pure or purified gold (Notebaart); refined gold (DCH) (1 Kgs 6:20)

זָהָב מִכְלוֹת   completely purified gold (Notebaart); perfect gold (DCH) (2 Chr 4:21)

חָרוּץ   gold (Prov 8:10 R)

יְרַקְרַק חָרוּץ   degraded, alloyed gold (Notebaart); greenness of gold (DCH) (Ps 68:14)

נִבְחָר חָרוּץ   best quality gold (Notebaart); refined gold (DCH) (Prov 8:10)

כֶּתֶם   gold (Song 5:11 R)

פָּז   gold (Notebaart); pure gold (DCH) (Song 5:11 R)

Silver

כֶּסֶף   silver; silver money, silver ore (DCH) (Job 28:1)

Lead

אֶבֶן הַבְּדִיל   plumb-line (Pritz) (Zech 4:10)

אֲנָךְ   lead, plumb-line (DCH) (Amos 7:8 R)

מִשְׁקָלֶת / מִשְׁקֹלֶת   plumb-line (Pritz) (Isa 28:17 R)

עֹפֶרֶת   lead, ore (Amzallag "Copper Metallurgy"); lead oxide (HALOT) (Num 31:22 R)

Iron

בַּרְזֶל   iron (Job 28:2)

מְטִיל בַּרְזֶל   iron bar (DCH) (Job 40:18 H)

Copper

נְחוּשָׁה / נְחֹשֶׁת   copper, bronze; perhaps money (DCH) (Job 6:12 H)

Other Metals

בְּדִיל   tin; antimony (DCH) (Isa 1:25 R)

חַשְׁמַל brass, electrum, metal; amber or bronze (DCH); "the intense pale yellow light radiated by metal in a molten state" (Amzallag "Copper Metallurgy") (Ezek 1:27 R)

Metallurgical Terms

בָּחוֹן assayer (Guillame) (Jer 6:27 H)

בֹּחַן graywacke (Noonan "Zion's Foundation"); testing, granite (DCH) (Isaiah 28:16 R)

גָּפְרִית brimstone (Amzallag "Copper Metallurgy"); sulphur (HALOT) (Job 18:15 R)

חֶלְאָה corrosion (Amzallag "Copper Metallurgy"); rust (DCH) (Ezek 24:6 R)

כִּבְשָׁן smelting furnace, kiln (Pritz) (Gen 19:28 R)

כּוּר smelting pot (for gold); smelting pot, furnace, crucible (DCH) (Prov 27:21 R)

מַפֻּחַ bellows (Notebaart, DCH) (Jer 6:29 H)

מַצְרֵף refiner, crucible (for silver); crucible (Guillame, DCH) (Prov 27:21 R)

סִיג / סוּג dross (Amzallag "Copper Metallurgy") (Ezek 22:18 R)

עֲלִיל crucible (Guillame) (Ps 12:7 H)

פַּעַם anvil (Pritz) (Isa 41:7)

צָרוֹף metal smelter, refiner (DCH) (Jer 6:29 H)

צָרַף goldsmith (Notebaart); metal smelter, refiner (DCH) (Isa 41:7)

קַנָּא rust (Amzallag "Furnace Remelting"); jealous (DCH) (Exod 20:25 R)

רָקִיעַ metallic firmament, plate (Amzallag "Copper Metallurgy") (Gen 1:17)

General Terms: Stones, Gems

אֶבֶן small stone, large stone for building, stele marking or commemorating things (Zhakevich) (Gen 11:3)

אֶבֶן יְקָרָה precious stone (Ezek 27:22)

אֶבֶן מַעֲמָסָה heavy stone (SDBH); stone of burden (DCH) (Zech 12:3)

אֶקְדָּח precious stone; beryl, red granite (DCH) (Isa 54:12 H)

גָּזִית cutting, hewn stone (DCH); ashlar (HALOT) (Exod 20:25)

מַצֵּבָה pillar, memorial stone (DCH) (Gen 28:18)

מִשְׁבְּצָה setting (for gem); setting of stones, chequer-work, plaiting (DCH) (Exod 28:13 R)

סֹחָרֶת stone, mineral, costly stone (Esth 1:6 H)

Stones

בַּהַט white marble, alabaster (CT); porphyry, marble (SDBH) (Esth 1:6 H)

דַּר alabaster; mother-of-pearl (Esth 1:6 H)

חַלָּמִישׁ flint, hard stone (Ps 114:8 R)

חָצָץ gravel (SDBH) (Prov 20:17 R)

טַחֹון millstone; hand-mill (Lam 5:13 H)

יַהֲלֹם onyx (black); diamond (?) (SDBH) (Ezek 28:13 R)

יָשְׁפֵה jasper (deep orange-red); jasper, quartz (DCH) (Exod 28:20 R)

כֵּף rock (SDBH); rock or mountain top (DCH) (Job 30:6 R)

סֹחָרֶת stone tile, used in paving (Esth 1:6 H)

פּוּר lot, small pebble used to decide questions, Purim (SDBH) (Esth 3:7 R)

פֶּלַח millstone, mill (Pritz) (Judg 9:53 R)

צוּר rock (SDBH); rock, cliff, rocky mountain, stone monument, rock (as metaphor) (DCH) (2 Sam 21:10)

צֹר / צַר flint (SDBH); pebble, flint, flint knife (HALOT) (Isa 5:28 R)

צְרֹור pebble (HCW); tiny grain (SDBH) (Amos 9:9 R)

רֵחַיִם millstones (dual); hand-mill (dual) (DCH) (Exod 11:5 R)

רֶכֶב millstone (Pritz) (Deut 24:6 R)

שְׁבוֹ agate (multicolor inside); red gem, perhaps beryl or agate (CT) (Exod 28:19 R)

שַׁיִשׁ / שֵׁשׁ marble (CT); white alabaster (SDBH) (1 Chr 29:2 R)

שַׁיִת white marble; thistles (not marble) (DCH) (Isa 9:17 R)

Gems

אֹדֶם garnet (yellow-red); carnelian (brown-red); red ruby (CT); chalcedony (Zhakevich); ruby, carnelian (SDBH); sardius (DCH) (Ezek 28:13 R)

אַחְלָמָה amethyst (violet); amethyst, reddish-brown or wine color (CT); jasper (Zhakevich) (Exod 28:19 R)

בָּרֶקֶת emerald (deep green); green stone, possibly emerald, malachite, or green beryl (CT) (Ezek 28:13 H)

גָּבִישׁ crystal (SDBH); rock crystal (DCH) (Job 28:18 H)

יָשְׁפֵה jade (nephrite; jadeite) (Zhakevich); jasper (SDBH); jasper, or perhaps a kind of quartz (DCH) (Exod 28:20 R)

כַּדְכֹּד red ruby; agate (DCH) (Isa 54:12 R)

לֶשֶׁם jacinth (red-orange) (Exod 28:19 R)

נֹפֶךְ red ruby, carbuncle; emerald; dark gem, possibly onyx or dark jasper (CT); malachite or turquoise (Zhakevich); garnet (DCH) (Exod 28:18 R)

סַפִּיר sapphire (blue); lapis lazuli (CT, DCH) (Lam 4:7)

פִּטְדָה topaz (yellow); yellow topaz or chrysolite (CT) (Exod 28:17 R)

רָאמוֹת black corals, or perhaps sea shells (plural) (DCH) (Job 28:18 R)

שֹׁהַם beryl (turquoise green); carnelian (Zhakevich); onyx (SDBH, DCH) (Gen 2:12)

שָׁמִיר gem, diamond; thorn (Isa 7:24 R)

תַּרְשִׁישׁ chrysolite (bright green); turqoise or another blue stone (CT); jasper (?), diamond (?) (Zhakevich); beryl (SDBH); topaz, beryl, or chrysolite (DCH) (Exod 28:20 R)

Minerals

בְּאֵר well, watering place, spring (SDBH) (Gen 16:14); tar pit, bitumen pit (Gen 14:10)

בֹּרִית potash, lye; alkali (HALOT) (Mal 3:2 R)

מְלֵחָה saltness, barrenness, salt flat (HCW) (Job 39:6 R)

נְצִיב pillar of salt (SDBH) (Gen 19:26)

נֶתֶר natron (Prov 25:20 R)

Pearls

בְּדֹלַח pearl (?), bdellium resin (DCH) (Num 11:7 R)

חָרוּז pearl bead; necklace (DCH) (Song 1:10 H)

פְּנִינִים pearls; rubies (DCH); corals (HALOT) (Lam 4:7 R)

COLORS

General Terms

כֵּהֶה   colorless, dull; dim (of eyes) (DCH) (Lev 13:39 R)

רִקְמָה   variegated color; embroidered cloth (SBDH) (Ezek 16:13)

Specific Colors

Black/Brown

אָמֹץ   chestnut (Hartley); piebald (of horses) (HALOT) (Zech 6:3, 6:7 R)

חוּם   swarthy, sunburnt; brown (color of sheep) (DCH) (Gen 30:32 R)

פּוּךְ   black powder used as eye makeup (SDBH); antimony, malachite (DCH) (Jer 4:30 R)

קָדַר   dressed in mourning attire (HALOT); be dark in mourning (DCH) (Jer 4:28)

קַדְרוּת   darkness of clouds (Hartley); darkness of mourning (Hartley) (Isa 50:3 H)

שָׁחוֹר   black; soot, blackness (HALOT) (Lam 4:8 H)

שָׁחַר   to become dark, charred, blackened, sooty (Hartley) (Job 30:30 H)

שְׁחַרְחֹר   swarthy, black (Song 1:6 H)

White

חוּר   to grow pale (SBDH); be white, pale (DCH) (Isa 29:22 H)

חֹר   white, pure, noble (Jer 39:6)

יֵרָקוֹן   paleness (of human complexion) (SDBH); rust, mildew (DCH) (Jer 30:6 R)

לָבָן   white, light-colored, bare (Lev 13:4)

לֹבֶן   whiteness (Hartley) (not in Hebrew Bible, only in Sir 43:18)

צַח   bright, sunny; glowing, shimmering (Hartley) (Jer 4:11 R)

צָחַח   to be bright, brilliant, glowing, radiant (Hartley) (Lam 4:7 H)

צָחַר   whiteness (of wool), sheen (Ezek 27:18 H)

Red

אדם   to become orange, red, brown, copper-colored (Hartley); to be red (DCH) (Lam 4:7)

אָדֹם/אָדֹם   rosy, red, ruddy; reddish brown (Num 19:2, Zech 1:8, 6:2), brown (Gen 25:30) (Hartley) (R)

אֲדַמְדָּם   reddish, bright red (Hartley R)

חַכְלִילִי   red wine color (CT) (Gen 49:12 H)

חַכְלִלוּת redness of eyes (CT); dullness of eyes (DCH) (Prov 23:29 H)

חָמוּץ violent, glaring red; blood color (CT) (Isa 63:1 H)

חמר to be flushed red (CT); to ferment (DCH) (Job 16:16 R)

כַּרְמִיל carmine, deep-red; scarlet, crimson (CT) (2 Chr 2:6 R)

לָבָן אֲדַמְדָּם pink of skin diseases (CT) (Lev 13:19 R)

לַהַב aflame, enflamed red (Isa 13:8) (SDBH); point/flash of spear (Job 39:23) (DCH)

פָּארוּר flushed red in health (of face) (SDBH); pinkish color of human complexion (Hartley) (Joel 2:6 R)

צָחֹר tawny, yellowish-red (HALOT) (Judg 5:10 H)

שָׁנִי crimson red (Exod 25:41)

שָׂרֹק yellow-red, tawny (CT) (Zech 1:8 R)

שָׁשַׁר red ochre, vermillion (bright red) (Ezek 23:14 R)

Purple

אַרְגָּוָן/אַרְגָּמָן purple, red-purple; dye made from various mollusk species (Hartley) (Exod 25:4)

תְּכֵלֶת violet, cerulean purple; dye from shellfish purpura hyacinthea (Hartley) (Exod 25:4)

Green

יָרָק green, yellow (CT); herbage, vegetables (DCH) (Deut 11:10 R)

יֶרֶק greenness, yellowness (CT) (Ps 37:2 R)

Yellow

יְרַקְרַק yellowish, greenish; yellow gold (HALOT) (Lev 14:37 R)

צָהֹב golden, yellow, blonde (Hartley); shiny (CT); red (DCH) (Lev 13:30 R)

צהב to be bright, shine, polish, burnish (Hartley); to gleam (of copper) (DCH); to shine like gold (SDBH) (Ezra 8:27 H)

צהל to cause something to shine by rubbing it with oil (of human face; association of happiness) (SDBH) (Ps 104:15 H)

Blue

כָּחָל dark blue (Hartley) (Ezek 23:40 H)

Spotted/Speckled

בָּרֹד mottled, blotched (Zech 6:3 R)

טְלָא spottled, colorful (Ezek 16:16 R)

צָבוּעַ speckled (of animals); hyena (?), bird of prey (?) (DCH) (Jer 12:9 H)

נָקֹד speckled (Gen 30:32 R)

עָקֹד striped, streaked (Gen 30:35 R)

TIME

Day: Morning to Night

Morning/Noon

אַשְׁמֹרֶת הַבֹּקֶר	morning watch (Miano) (Exod 14:24)
בֹּקֶר	morning, dawn (Gen 1:5)
בִּתְרוֹן	morning (SDBH) (2 Sam 2:29 H)
מִשְׁחָר	dawn (Ps 110:3 H)
נְהָרָה	daylight (Job 3:4 H)
צָהֳרַיִם	noon, midday (1 Kgs 18:29)
שַׁחַר	dawn (Gen 19:15)

Evening

אֶמֶשׁ	twilight, evening (SDBH) (Job 30:3 R)
מָבוֹא	sunset, west (Josh 1:4)
נֶשֶׁף	twilight (Ps 119:147)
עֲלָטָה	dusk, twilight (Gen 15:17 R)
עֶרֶב	evening (Gen 1:5)

Night

אַשְׁמוּרָה	night watch (SDBH) (Exod 14:24 R)
אַשְׁמֹרֶת הַתִּיכוֹנָה	middle watch (Miano) (Judg 7:19)
לַיְלָה/לֵיל	night (Exod 12:42)

General Terms: Days/Week

אֶמֶשׁ	yesterday; evening (DCH); last night (SDBH) (Gen 19:34)
אֶתְמוֹל / תְּמוֹל	yesterday, ago (Exod 5:14)
יוֹם	day; 24-hour span (Miano) (Gen 1:5)
יוֹמָם	daily (Jer 15:9)
מָחָר	tomorrow (Gen 30:33)
מָחֳרָת	tomorrow, next day (Num 11:32)
שָׁבוּעַ	week (Gen 29:27)
שֶׁבַע	week; seven (DCH) (Gen 5:7)
שִׁלְשׁוֹם	day before yesterday (Prov 22:20)

General Terms: Time

Past

אֱשׁוּן	starting time; period of time (SDBH); beginning (DCH) (Prov 20:20 H)
דּוֹר	generation; roughly 28 years (Miano) (Isa 51:9)
יָשָׁן	old (SDBH) (Lev 25:22 R)
כְּבָר	formerly (Eccl 1:10 R)

קְדוּמִים ancient (SDBH) (Judg 5:21 H)
קַדְמֹנִי former, past, old (SDBH) (1 Sam 24:14)
רֵאשִׁית first, beginning (Gen 1:1)

Now

אֵפוֹא / אֵפוֹ now, then, here (Gen 27:37)
אֹפֶן right time, right moment (SDBH); occasion (DCH) (Prov 25:11 H)
זְמָן set time, appointment (Eccl 3:1 R)
עֵת time, now, when (Neh 9:28)
עַתָּה now, at this time (2 Sam 24:16)
עִתִּי timely; ready (DCH) (Lev 16:21 H)
פִּתְאָם / פִּתְאוֹם instantly; suddenness (DCH) (2 Chr 29:36)
פֶּתַע moment, wink, instant (Num 6:9 R)
רֶגַע wink, short space of time (Ps 30:6)

Future

אַחֲרִית future (Prov 23:18)
יֶתֶר rest of time (SDBH) (Isa 38:10)
מוֹעֵד appointment, fixed time (Jer 8:7)
נֶצַח duration, ever, everlasting rest (Jer 15:18)
עוֹלָם everlasting, eternity; perpetuity (Barr) (Isa 44:7)
צְפִירָה moment of doom (SDBH); doom, cycle, climax (DCH) (Ezek 7:7 R)

Month/Year

חַג feast, festival (SDBH) (Exod 10:9)
חַג הָאָסִף Feast of the Harvest (Borowski *Agriculture*) (Exod 23:16)
חַג הַמַּצּוֹת Feast of Unleavened Bread, Passover (Borowski *Agriculture*) (Exod 23:15)
חַג סֻכּוֹת Festival of Sukkoth; Feast of Booths (Borowski *Agriculture*) (Lev 23:34)
חַג שָׁבֻעֹת Feast of Weeks (Borowski *Agriculture*) (Exod 34:22)
חֹדֶשׁ month, New Moon Festival (SDBH) (Gen 7:11)
יֶרַח month (Exod 2:2)
כֶּסֶא full moon (Prov 7:20 R)
פּוּרִים Purim Festival (SDBH) (Esth 9:26 R)
פֶּסַח Passover (Exod 12:11)
צֵאת הַשָּׁנָה "exit of the year," end of the liturgical year (Miano) (Exod 23:16)
שָׁנָה year (Gen 5:4)
תְּקוּפָה circuit; end (of year) (SDBH) (Exod 34:22 R)

תְּקוּפַת הַשָּׁנָה "at the coming round of the year," the end of the civil year (Miano) (Exod 34:22)

Calendar

נִיסָן Nisan (1); March/April (SDBH) (Neh 2:1 R)

זִו Ziv (2), April/May (SDBH) (1 Kgs 6:1 R)

סִיוָן Sivan (3); May/June (SDBH) (Esth 8:9 H)

תַּמּוּז [Tammuz] (4)

אָב / אָבִיב Ab (5); July/August (SDBH) (Exod 13:4 R)

אֱלוּל Elul (6); August/September (SDBH) (Neh 6:15 H)

אֵיתָנִים Ethanim (7); September/October (SDBH) (1 Kgs 8:2 H)

בּוּל Bul (8); October/November (SDBH) (1 Kgs 6:38 H)

כִּסְלֵו Kislev (9); November/December (SDBH) (Neh 1:1 R)

טֵבֵת Teveth (10); mid-December to mid-January (SDBH) (Esth 2:16 H)

שְׁבָט Shevat (11); January/February (SDBH) (Zech 1:7 H)

אֲדָר Adar (12); February/March (SDBH) (Esth 3:7 R)

Seasons

דַּיִשׁ threshing time (Lev 26:5 H)

חָרִישׁ season of ploughing (Gen 45:6 R)

חֹרֶף autumn, harvest time; winter (SDBH); winter (DCH) (Gen 8:22 R)

סְתָיו winter (Song 2:11 H)

קַיִץ harvest; summer (SDBH) (Gen 8:22)

קָצִיר harvest (DCH) (Jer 8:20)

ANIMALS

General Terms

בְּהֵמָה   animal (Gen 1:26)

חַי/חַיָּה   living-creature, beast (Ezek 1:5)

טֶרֶף/טְרֵפָה   devoured, eaten (of animals) (ELT); savaged beast, one torn apart by other beasts (DCH) (Exod 22:30)

נְבֵלָה   carcass, corpse (of animals) (ELT); corpse of animal, human, or idol (DCH) (Deut 28:26)

פַּרְסָה   hoof (Exod 10:26)

רֶמֶשׂ   creeping things, crawling; small, unclean creatures, esp. reptiles (Hope); esp. insects and reptiles (DCH) (Ps 148:10)

שֶׁרֶץ   swarming things, teem; small, swarming mammals, reptiles, or flying insects (DCH) (Gen 7:21)

Birds

General

אֶבְרָה   wing of bird (DCH) (Deut 32:11 R)

אֶפְרֹחַ   nestling (SDBH); young bird (HALOT) (Deut 22:6 R)

בֵּיצָה   egg (of bird) (DCH) (Deut 22:6 R)

עוֹף   birds, fowl; flying birds or insects (DCH) (Lev 11:20)

עַיִט   bird of prey, hawk (Jer 12:9 R)

קֵן   bird's nest; nestlings, brood (DCH) (Obad 4)

תֻּכִּיִּים   exotic birds, parrots (ELT); peacocks, or perhaps poultry, or apes (DCH) (1 Kgs 10:22 R)

Specific Birds (Listed in English Order)

Various B–C

קִפּוֹד   bittern, bustard; porcupine (?); hedgehog, porcupine, or owl (DCH) (Isa 34:11 R)

שֶׂכְוִי   cock, rooster (Job 38:36 H)

זַרְזִיר   cock, hen, chicken; "girt of loins"; strong, girded, perhaps greyhound or cockerel (DCH) (Prov 30:31 H)

שָׁלָךְ   cormorant (DCH); osprey (Hope); owl (ELT) (Lev 11:17 R)

עָגוּר   crane, swallow (Jer 8:7 R)

Doves/Geese

יוֹנָה   dove, pigeon (Gen 8:11)

תֹּר/תוֹר   dove, ring-dove; turtledove (DCH) (Jer 8:7)

גּוֹזָל   young-dove; nestling of any bird species (Hope); chick (ELT) (Gen 15:9 R)

בַּרְבֻּרִים   geese; cuckoos, young chickens (HALOT) (1 Kgs 5:3 H)

Hawks/Falcons

נֵץ   kestrel; falcon (HALOT); sparrow, hawk (Hope) (Lev 11:16 R)

אַיָּה   falcon, buzzard, harrier (screamer) (Lev 11:14 R)

אֲנָפָה   heron; un-kosher bird, plover or cormorant (HALOT) (Lev 11:19 R)

דָּאָה / רָאָה   kite, hawk; falcon (ELT) (Lev 11:14 H)

דַּיָּה   kite, hawk, falcon, vulture (Deut 14:13 R)

רָחָם   osprey, fisher-hawk; Egyptian vulture (Hope, ELT); carrion-vulture or osprey (DCH) (Lev 11:18 R)

Various H

דּוּכִיפַת   hoopoe (orange crown) (Deut 14:18 R)

Ostriches

יָעֵן   ostrich (Lam 4:3 H)

בַּת־הַיַּעֲנָה   ostrich; eagle owl (Hope); literally "daughter of the desert" (DCH) (Lev 11:16 R)

רְנָנִים   ostriches; female ostriches (HALOT) (Job 39:13 H)

Owls

תַּחְמָס   short-eared owl; falcon (ELT); perhaps nighthawk or male ostrich (DCH) (Lev 11:16 R)

כּוֹס   tawny owl, little owl; little owl (UBS); screech-owl, little owl (HALOT) (Deut 14:16 R)

יַנְשׁוּף   great owl; tawny owl (Hope); eagle owl, long-eared owl, bee-eater (UBS); screech owl, unclean bird (DCH) (Isa 34:11 R)

תִּנְשֶׁמֶת   barn owl (Hope); white owl, or perhaps little owl or water hen, or chameleon (DCH) (Lev 11:30 R)

לִילִית   night-hag, screech owl (?); tawny owl (unclear) (Hope); Lilith, or perhaps nightjar (DCH) (Isa 34:14 H)

Various P–S

קוֹרֵא / קְרָא   partridge (caller) (Jer 17:11 R)

קָאַת   pelican; jackdaw, owl (Hope); pelican, also perhaps hawk or vulture (DCH) (Zeph 2:14 R)

שְׂלָו   quail (Exod 16:13 R)

עֹרֵב   raven; rook (DCH) (1 Kgs 17:6)

שַׁחַף   sea gull; tern; wood owl or gull (ELT); also possibly bat (HALOT) (Lev 11:16 R)

צִפּוֹר   sparrow, little bird; general term for small birds about the size of a sparrow (Hope); (Job 40:29)

חֲסִידָה   stork (the "kind" bird); "considered to be affectionate to its young, in contrast to the ostrich" (UBS); possibly heron (HALOT) (Zech 5:9 R)

דְּרוֹר   swallow; dove; swallow, martin (Hope) (Ps 84:4 R)

סוּס / סִיס   swift; possibly golden oriole (DCH) (Jer 8:7 R)

Vultures/Eagles

נֶשֶׁר eagle; general term for large bird of prey but also specifically large vulture, large eagle (Hope) (Exod 19:4)

פֶּרֶס Arrians vulture; eagle, bearded vulture (Hope) (Deut 14:12 R)

עׇזְנִיׇּה bearded vulture; eagle; black vulture (Hope); or osprey (DCH) (Lev 11:13 R)

Cattle

אַבִּיר "strong, mighty" bull; stallion (SDBH) (1 Sam 21:8)

אַלּוּף/אֶלֶף bullock; cattle, oxen (DCH) (Ps 144:14 R)

בְּהֵמׇה cattle, animal; domestic animals, livestock (SDBH) (Ps 104:14)

בְּעִיר cattle, livestock; beasts of burden (DCH) (Gen 45:17 R)

בׇּקׇר ox, cattle, herd; usually cattle but may include sheep or goats (Hope); large cattle (ELT) (1 Kgs 7:25)

מִקְנֶה livestock, cattle; usually cows and sheep but also camels, horses, asses (DCH) (Exod 9:3)

מְרִיא fattened calf, fatling; stall-fed calf, reserved for sacrifice (Hope) (Isa 1:11 R)

עֵגֶל calf; male calf, young bull (DCH) (Lev 9:2)

עֶגְלׇה heifer (Deut 21:3)

פַּר/פָּר young bull, bullock; young bull reserved for sacrifice (Hope); bull, irrespective of age, offered for sacrifice (DCH) (Ps 22:13)

פׇּרׇה cow; young bull reserved for sacrifice (Hope) (Num 19:2)

רְאֵם wild ox (Job 39:9 R)

שׁוֹר single head of cattle, bullock; ox (ELT); Taurus (in Zodiac) (DCH) (Lev 4:10)

תְּאוֹ wild bull; antelope (DCH); oryx (Hope); water buffalo (ELT) (Deut 14:5 R)

תּוֹעֲפֹת (bull) horns (pl.) (Num 23:22 R)

Sheep, Goats

Sheep

אַיִל ram; leader of nation (DCH) (Lev 23:18)

אֵיל הַמִּלֻּאִים fattened ram (ELT) (Lev 8:29)

אַלְיׇה sheep's tail; fat tail of sacrificial ram (DCH); fat tail of sheep (HALOT) (Exod 29:22 R)

טׇלֶה lamb; very young, unweaned lamb (Hope) (1 Sam 7:9 R)

יוֹבֵל ram's horn, ram (Josh 6:5)

כֶּבֶשׂ lamb (male); sheep (ELT); young ram, usually sacrificial animal (HALOT) (Lev 4:32)

כִּבְשׇׂה ewe-lamb (female) (Lev 14:10 R)

כַּר   ram; ram, pasture (ELT); young ram, battering ram (DCH)
(Amos 6:4)

מֵחִים   fattened ram (ELT); fatling of sheep (Isa 5:17 R)

עֵדֶר   flock (sheep, goats); "a combination of flocks of domestic
animals" (Hope) (Song 4:1)

צֹנֶה/צֹאן   flock; a group within an עֵדֶר (Hope); small cattle (ELT)
(Gen 30:32)

רָחֵל   ewe (female adult) (Song 6:6 R)

שֶׂה   member of flock, sheep, goat; young lamb (ELT); small
livestock beast (DCH) (Gen 30:32)

Goats

אַקּוֹ   wild goat, ibex, slender; mountain goat (SDBH) (Deut 14:5 H)

גְּדִי   kid-goat; female kid-goat גְּדִיָּה (Hope) (Judg 6:19)

זֶמֶר   mountain goat, mountain sheep (leap); wild ungulate (ELT)
(Deut 14:5 H)

יָעֵל   male wild-goat, ibex; mountain goat (SDBH) (Ps 104:18 R)

יַעֲלָה   female wild-goat, ibex (Prov 5:19 H)

עֵז   she-goat; goat hair, the She-goat (constellation) (DCH)
(Gen 27:9)

עַתּוּד   he-goat; dominant male goat in flock (Hope); ram (ELT);
male goat, usually as sacrifice (DCH) (Gen 31:10)

צָפִיר/צְפִיר   he-goat; possibly castrated male (Hope); kid goat (ELT)
(2 Chr 29:21 R)

שָׂעִיר   hairy goat (shaggy); young goat (ELT); he-goat, or hairy
demon in shape of he-goat (Isa 13:21)

שְׂעִירָה   hairy she-goat (Lev 4:28 R)

תַּיִשׁ   he-goat, billy-goat; lit. "the one that butts" (Hope) (Gen 32:15 R)

Enclosures/Troughs

אֵבוּס   feeding trough, manger, stall, crib (Prov 14:4 R)

אֲבֵרָה   manger, crib, stall; wing (DCH) (Job 39:13 R)

אֻרְוָה   manger, crib, stall; herding place; stable (HALOT) (1 Kgs 5:6 R)

בָּצְרָה   enclosure for sheep or goats (DCH) (Mic 2:12)

גִּדְרֹת צֹאן   pens, enclosures (ELT) (Num 32:16)

מִכְלָא   sheepfold, enclosure; pen for sheep and goats (HALOT)
(Ps 78:70 R)

מְלוּנָה   watchman's hut (in field) (Isa 24:20 R)

מַרְבֵּה   stall; fattening (DCH) (Sir 38:26 R)

מַרְבֵּץ   fold for sheep, lair for wild animals (HALOT) (Ezek 25:5 R)

רְהָטִים   troughs (ELT) (Gen 30:38 R)

רֶפֶת   stable, stall for cattle (Hab 3:17 H)

שִׁקֲתוֹת הַמַּיִם   watering troughs (ELT) (Gen 30:38)

Animal Husbandry Tools

דָּרְבָן	goad (Borowski *Agriculture*) (1 Sam 13:21 R)
חָח	nose hook (ELT (2 Kgs 19:28 R)
יַלְקוּט	bag/pouch of a shepherd (Pritz) (1 Sam 17:40 H)
כְּלֵי הַבָּקָר	yoke (Borowski *Agriculture*) (2 Sam 24:22)
כְּלֵי הָרֹעִים	bag/pouch of a shepherd (Pritz) (1 Sam 17:40)
כַּר הַגָּמָל	saddle for camel (ELT) (Gen 31:34)
מוֹטָה	yoke (Borowski *Agriculture*); bar of yoke, yoke (DCH) (Nah 1:13)
מוֹסֵר	rein, fetter (ELT) (Jer 5:5 R)
מַחְסוֹם	muzzle (Pritz) (Ps 39:1 H)
מִשְׁעֶנֶת	rod, club, shepherd's staff (Pritz) (Exod 21:19)
מַלְמָד	goad (Borowski *Agriculture*) (Judg 3:31 H)
מַקֵּל	rod, club, shepherd's staff (Pritz) (Gen 32:10)
מֶתֶג	bridle (ELT); muzzle (DCH) (Ps 32:9 R)
עֲבֹת / עֲבוֹת	reins (ELT); cord, branch (DCH) (Isa 5:18)
עֹל	yoke (Deut 21:3)
צְרוֹר	bundle, parcel, pouch; money pouch, purse (כלי) (Song 1:13 R)
רֶסֶן	bit (ELT); halter for horse or mule (DCH) (Isa 30:28 R)
שֵׁבֶט	rod, club, shepherd's staff (Pritz) (Exod 21:20)
שֹׁטֵט	whip, scourge (Pritz) (Josh 23:13 H)

Pasturage

דֹּבֶר	pasture (Mic 2:12 R)
מַדְבָּר	pasturage, wilderness; desert (Exod 3:1)
מִרְעֶה	feeding place, pasture; haunt (of wild animals); steppe, wilderness, desert, place of wild animals and birds (DCH) (Joel 1:18)
מַרְעִית	pasturage; flock; shepherding (Jer 23:1)
נָאָה	pasture, meadow, abode; pleasant place, oasis (DCH) (Ps 65:13)
נַהֲלֹל	pasture, watering-place (Isa 7:19 H)
גֶּוֶה	abode of flocks, meadow, habitation (Exod 15:13)

Horses, Mules, Asses

Horses

אַבִּיר	"mighty" (horse) (+bull); possibly war-horses, so "charger" or "steed" (Hope) (Judg 5:22)
סוּס	horse (Exod 14:23)
עִקְּבֵי־סוּס	horses' hooves (ELT) (Judg 5:22)

פָּרָשׁ horse, horseman; warhorse and rider as a unit, cavalry (Hope); charioteer (DCH) (Jer 4:29)

רֶכֶשׁ horses, charioting; fast, swift horse (Hope); draft horse (ELT); steeds (DCH); team of horses, post horses (HALOT) (Esth 8:10 R)

Mules

פֶּרֶד mule; mule (*Equus hemionus*) (Way) (Isa 66:20)

פִּרְדָּה she-mule; mule (*Equus hemionus*) (Way) (1 Kgs 1:38 R)

Asses

אָתוֹן she-ass; female donkey, "jenny" (Way) (1 Sam 9:3)

חֲמוֹר male-ass (red, tawny); general term for donkey (Way) (Gen 22:3)

עַיִר (male) young ass, ass colt, foal; male equid (Way); young donkey (ELT) (Isa 30:24 R)

עָרוֹד wild ass, onager; Nubian wild ass (Hope) (Job 39:5 H)

פֶּרֶא wild ass, onager; onager (Hope); less probably zebra (DCH) (Hos 8:9)

Large Mammals

Various

בְּהֵמוֹת hippo; elephant, Behemoth (SDBH); less probably hippopotamus (DCH) (Job 40:15)

דֹּב bear; Syrian brown bear (SDBH) (Lam 3:10)

דִּישׁוֹן antelope (leaper); addax, waterbuck, defassa, kob (SDBH); wild ungulate (ELT); ibex, or perhaps pygarg (DCH); bison (HALOT) (Deut 14:5 H)

חֲזִיר swine, pig; wild pig (SDBH); can be either domestic or wild pig (Hope); wild boar (Hope, HALOT) (Lev 11:7 R)

נָמֵר leopard; panther (HALOT) (Isa 11:6 R)

צְבִי/צְבִיָּה gazelle; doe (ELT); deer (DCH) (Song 4:5 R)

Camel

בֶּכֶר young camel (male) (Isa 60:6 H)

בִּכְרָה young she-camel; young she-camel in heat (Hope) (Jer 2:23 H)

גָּמָל camel (1 Sam 15:3)

כִּרְכָּרָה riding camel, a dromedary; fast-running female camel (HALOT) (Isa 66:20 H)

Primate

קוֹף monkey, ape, baboon (1 Kgs 10:22 R)

תֻּכִּיִּים baboon, monkey; vervet monkey (SDBH); peacocks, or perhaps poultry or apes (DCH); baboon (HALOT) (2 Chr 9:21 R)

Deer

אַיָל   deer (fallow, large); roe deer (ELT) (1 Kgs 5:3)

אַיָלָה / אַיֶּלֶת   hind, doe (Hab 3:19)

אֹמֶר   fawn (?) (SDBH) (Gen 49:21 H)

יַחְמוּר   roe-deer; Red Hartebeest (antelope); Bubal Hartebeest (Hope); fallow deer (UBS); roebuck (DCH) (Deut 14:5 R)

עֹפֶר   young hart, stag (Song of Solomon); young deer, fawn stag, or perhaps ibex (DCH) (Song 4:5 R)

Hyena

צָבוּעַ   hyena; bird of prey (DCH) (Jer 12:9 H)

צִיִּים   hyenas (?) (Hope) (Jer 50:39 R)

Lions

אֲרִי   lion; male lion (Clines "Misapprehensions"); African lion (HALOT) (2 Kgs 17:25)

אַרְיֵה   lion; female lion (Hope) (Gen 49:9)

גוּר / גּוֹר   cub (of lion) (Ezek 19:3 R)

כְּפִיר   young lion (DCH, HALOT); not specifically young, but still male lion (Clines); hunting/killing lion (Hope) (Ezek 19:2)

לֶבָא   male lion (Clines "Misapprehensions") (Ps 57:5 H)

לְבָאֹת   female lions (DCH) (Nah 2:13 H)

לָבִיא   male lion (Clines "Misapprehensions") (Nah 2:12)

לְבִיָּה   female lion (Nah 2:13 R)

לַיִשׁ   lion, old lion; strong lion (SDBH); male lion (Clines "Misapprehensions"); lion in its prime, not old lion (Hope) (Isa 30:6 R)

שַׁחַל   lion; male lion (Hope); lion-cub (HALOT) (Job 28:8 R)

Dog-Like

אֹחַ   animal that produces sounds symbolizing death and destruction, jackal (?) (SDBH); owl (DCH) (Isa 13:21 H)

אִי   jackal, howler (Isa 13:22 R)

זְאֵב   wolf (Gen 49:27 R)

כֶּלֶב   dog (1 Kgs 14:11)

נָבַח   to bark (Isa 56:10 H)

כַּלְבֵי צֹאן   sheep dog (ELT) (Job 30:1 R)

שׁוּעָל   fox, jackal (Lam 5:18 R)

תַּן / תַּנָּה   fox, jackal; a type of snake or dragon/sea monster in early Hebrew but became term for jackal in later Hebrew (Hope); jackal (HALOT) (Deut 32:33)

Small Mammals

אַרְנֶבֶת hare (Lev 11:6 R)

חֹלֶד weasel, mole; mongoose (Hope) (Lev 11:29 H)

חֲפַרְפָּרָה mole; mole rat (Hope); mole, shrew, perhaps bat (DCH) (Isa 2:20 H)

עֲטַלֵּף bat (Lev 11:19 R)

עַכְבָּר mouse; rat (Hope); jerboa (HALOT) (Isa 66:17 R)

שָׁפָן rock badger, hyrax (Lev 11:5 R)

Lizards/Reptiles

אֲנָקָה gecko; reptile (ELT) (Ps 79:11 R)

חֹמֶט skink (desert brown lizard) (Lev 11:30 H)

כֹּחַ land crocodile; monitor lizard (Hope) (Lev 11:30 H)

לְטָאָה lizard; reptile (ELT); lacertid lizard (SDBH); gecko (HALOT) (Lev 11:30 H)

צָב horn-tailed lizard; thorn-tailed lizard (DCH) (Lev 11:29 H)

צְפַרְדֵּעַ / צְפַדֵּעַ frog; (plague of) frogs (SDBH) (Exod 8:5)

שַׁחַל lizard, usually lion (DCH) (Ps 91:13)

תִּנְשֶׁמֶת chameleon; white owl, little owl, water hen, perhaps chameleon (DCH) (Lev 11:18 R)

Snakes

אֶפְעֶה carpet viper (hissing) (Isa 59:5 R)

בֵּיצָה egg (of viper) (DCH) (Isa 59:5 R)

לִוְיָתָן Leviathan; mythical crocodile monster (?) (Hope); giant crocodile, giant sea monster (SDBH) (Ps 104:26 R)

נָחָשׁ snake; serpent, perhaps Leviathan (DCH) (Gen 3:1)

פֶּתֶן asp, cobra (Ps 58:5 R)

צֶפַע cat snake (ailurophis vivax); cobra (Hope); poisonous snake (DCH) (Isa 14:29 H)

קִפּוֹד arrow-snake (leaps); hedgehog, porcupine, or owl (DCH) (Is 34:11 R)

קִפּוֹז arrow snake, dart snake (Isa 34:15 H)

שְׁפִיפֹן horned adder; viper (Hope); horned viper (DCH); horned snake (HALOT) (Gen 49:17 H)

שָׂרָף poisonous snake; viper (Hope); carpet viper (SDBH); venomous snake, cobra (DCH) (Num 21:6 R)

תַּנִּין serpent; sea monster (Ezek 29:3)

Fish/Aquatic

דָּג/דָּגָה   fish; fish (collective) (ELT) (Jonah 2:2)

תַּחַשׁ   manatee (dugong), dolphin (?); crocodile (?) (ELT); dolphin, porpoise (DCH) (Num 4:6)

Mollusks

שַׁבְלוּל   snail (Ps 58:9 H)

שְׁחֵלֶת   onycha (mollusk) (aromatic) (Exod 30:34 H)

Arthropods: Insects, Worms, Etc.

דְּבוֹרָה   bee (Deut 1:44 R)

זְבוּב   fly (Eccl 10:1 R)

כֵּן/כִּנָּם   gnat, mosquito; lice (ELT); louse, maggot (DCH) (Isa 51:6 R)

נְמָלָה   ant (Prov 6:6 R)

סָס   moth (Isa 51:8 H)

עַכָּבִישׁ   spider (Job 8:14 R)

עֲלוּקָה   leech (Prov 30:15 H)

עַקְרָב   scorpion (Deut 8:15 R)

עָרֹב   flier, swarm; swarms of flies (DCH) (Exod 8:20 R)

עָשׁ   moth (Isa 50:9 R)

פַּרְעֹשׁ   flea (1 Sam 26:20 R)

צִרְעָה   hornet (Exod 23:28 R)

קֶרֶץ   gadfly (Jer 46:20 H)

רִמָּה   maggot; worm (DCH) (Exod 16:24 R)

שְׂמָמִית   spider; gecko (SDBH); lizard (DCH) (Prov 30:28 H)

תּוֹלָע   worm (Lam 4:5 R)

Locusts

אַרְבֶּה   locust (winged stage) (Exod 10:14)

גֹּבַי   locust; swarm of locusts (DCH) (Amos 7:1 R)

גָּזָם   cutter, locust, caterpillar; locust grub (DCH) (Joel 1:4 R)

חָנָב   locust, crawling nymph, caterpillar; grasshopper (Hope) (2 Chr 7:13 R)

חָסִיל   hopper locust, ravager; cockroach; grasshopper (Hope) (1 Kgs 8:37 R)

חַרְגֹּל   locust, leaping insect (Lev 11:22 H)

יֶלֶק   grub (unwinged stage) (Ps 105:34 R)

סָלְעָם   locust; perhaps long-headed locust or bald locust (DCH) (Lev 11:22 H)

צְלָצַל   whirring locust; cricket; onomatopoeic word representing the sound of an insect swarm (Hope) (Deut 28:42 H)

Snares and Traps

General

חֶבֶל   rope, noose (Pritz) (Job 18:10)

יָקוּשׁ   trap, snare (Pritz); game hunter (DCH) (Ps 91:3 R)

כְּלוּב   bird trap; basket; basket for fruit, bird-cage (DCH) (Jer 5:27 R)

מוֹקֵשׁ   snare, noose; striker, bait, decoy (DCH) (Amos 3:5)

מָזוֹר   trap, snare (Pritz) (Obad 7 H)

מִכְמָר/מִכְמֹר   hunter's net, snare (Isa 51:20 R)

מַלְכֹּדֶת   snare, trap (Job 18:10 H)

מָצוֹד   snare, net (Eccl 7:26 R)

סוּגַּר   cage, wooden collar (Pritz); neck collar (DCH) (Ezek 19:9 H)

פַּח   net, snare; trap (DCH) (Isa 24:17)

פַּחַת   pit, trap; ravine (DCH) (2 Sam 17:9)

צַמִּים   snares (Pritz) (Job 18:9 R)

רֶשֶׁת   net, trap (Prov 1:17)

שְׂבָכָה   pitfall, pit trap (Pritz); network, toils, window-lattice or architectural ornamentation (DCH) (Job 18:8)

שׁוּחָה/שַׁחַת/שִׁיחָה   trap, snare (Pritz) (Prov 22:14 R)

Fishing Equipment

חַכָּה   fishing implement (ELT); fish-hook (DCH) (Isa 19:8 R)

חֵרֶם   hunter's net; fishing net (ELT) (Eccl 7:26 R)

מִכְמֶרֶת   fishing-net, dragnet (Hab 1:15 R)

מַשָּׂע   fishing spear, harpoon (Pritz); missile, dart, arrow, or other weapon (DCH) (Job 41:26 R)

סִיר דּוּגָה   (fish) hook (Pritz) (Amos 4:2 R)

צִלְצַל דָּגִים   fishing harpoon, fishing spear (ELT) (Job 40:31 H)

צִנּוֹת   (fish) hooks (Pritz) (Amos 4:2 H)

שְׂכּוֹת   fishing spears, harpoons (Pritz) (Job 41:7 H)

FLORA

── Trees: General and Specific ──

General

אֶזְרָח native tree (SDBH); cedar (Koops) (Ps 37:35 H)

חֹרֶשׁ forest, wood (Ezek 31:3 R)

יַעַר wood, forest, thicket (2 Sam 18:8)

עֵץ tree (Exod 15:25)

Specific Trees

אֵלָה/אַלָּה terebinth (Isa 1:29 H)

אֵלוֹן/אַלּוֹן oak; terebinth (DCH) (Isa 44:14 R)

אַלְמֻגִּים/אַלְגּוּמִים sandlewood, algum/almug (timber); juniper tree (SDBH); sandalwood (Koops) (1 Kgs 10:11 R)

אֶרֶז cedar; Phoenician juniper (Koops) (Lev 14:4)

אֹרֶן laurel (bay-tree) (not pine!); pine tree; fir tree; cedar; laurel (SDBH); pine (Sherwin) (Isa 44:14 H)

אֵשֶׁל tamarisk (Gen 21:33 R)

אֲשֻׁרִים/תְּאַשּׁוּר box tree (Ezek 27:6)

בָּכָא poplar; balsam tree, aspen tree, poplar (SDBH) (2 Sam 5:23–24 R)

בְּרוֹת/בְּרוֹשׁ cypress, fir, juniper; Grecian juniper (Koops) (2 Sam 6:5 H)

גֹּפֶר gopher; cypress (Koops) (Gen 6:14 H)

הָבְנִים/הוֹבְנִים/הָבְנִי ebony (Ezek 27:15 H)

הֲדַס myrtle (Neh 8:15 R)

לִבְנֶה styrax (white flower); white poplar (SDBH); styrax (Koops) (Gen 30:37 R)

נַחַל palm-tree; date palm (DCH) (Num 24:6 R)

עֵץ שֶׁמֶן "trees of oil," e.g., olive oil, hence "olive tree" (DCH); Aleppo pine (Neh 8:15 H)

עֲרָבִים poplar; willow (pl. only) (Ps 137:2 R)

עָרִיץ laurel (?) (Koops); terrifying (DCH) (Ps 37:35 H)

עַרְמוֹן plane tree (Gen 30:37)

עַרְעֵר/עַרְעָר juniper, tamarisk (DCH) (Jer 17:6 H)

צַפְצָפָה willow (Ezek 17:5 H)

קִדָּה cassia bark (aromatic) (Exod 30:24 R)

קָנֶה calamus reed (Harrison); sweet cane, ginger grass (Koops) (Ezek 27:19)

קְנֵה הַטּוֹב calamus reed, sweet cane, ginger grass (Koops) (Jer 6:20)

קָנֶה־בֹּשֶׂם calamus reed, sweet cane, ginger grass (Koops) (Exod 30:23)

קְצִיעוֹת/קְצִיעָה cassia (Ps 45:9 H)

רֹתֶם broom tree (SDBH) (1 Kgs 19:4 R)

שִׁטָּה   acacia (Exod 25:5)

שֶׁמֶן   oil tree; wild olive; oleaster (SDBH) (1 Kgs 6:23)

שֶׁמֶן שָׂשׂוֹן   "oil of gladness," possibly cassia, Indian orris, or Sausurea lappa (Harrison) (Ps 45:8)

שִׁקְמָה   sycamore (1 Kgs 10:27 R)

תְּאַשּׁוּר   cypress; fir; juniper (SDBH) (Isa 41:19 R)

תִּדְהָר   Brutian pine; Laurustinus shrub; cypress (Koops) (Isa 41:19 R)

תִּרְזָה   stone pine; holm tree; a type of oak (Sherwin); holm tree (DCH) (Isa 44:14 H)

Grasses

דֶּשֶׁא   sprout, grass; green vegetation, grass (SDBH) (Gen 1:11)

חָצִיר   grass; leek (Num 11:5 H)

חֲשַׁשׁ   dry grass (Isa 5:24 R)

מִרְעֶה   grass, pasture (Koops) (Gen 47:4)

עֵשֶׂב   grass (Gen 1:11–12)

Reeds

אֵבֶה   papyrus; reeds (SDBH) (Job 9:26 H)

אַגְמוֹן   cattail, bulrush (Job 41:12 R)

אָחוּ   reed, marshy grass (Gen 41:2 R)

גֹּמֶא   bulrush, papyrus (Exod 2:3 R)

סוּף   (sea of) reeds; cattails, bulrushes (SDBH) (Exod 2:3)

קָנֶה   reed, stem, rod (1 Kgs 14:15)

Flowers and Plants

בָּאְשָׁה   weed, stinky weed (Koops) (Job 31:40 H)

גַּלְגַּל   tumbleweed (Ps 83:14)

גֶּפֶן סְדֹם   "vine of Sodom" = colocynth, a poisonous plant (Koops) (Deut 32:32)

חֲבַצֶּלֶת   narcissus, "rose"; "rose of Sharon," mountain tulip (Koops) (Song 2:1)

חַלָּמוּת   purslane; juice of purslane / mallows (SDBH) (Job 6:6 H)

יָרוֹק   green (leaves, plants) (SDBH); "greens," vegetables (Job 39:8 H)

יֶרֶק   grass, green (Koops) (Gen 1:30 R)

לַעֲנָה   wormwood (Deut 29:17 R)

מַלּוּחַ   saltbush; saltwort; mallow (SDBH) (Job 30:4 H)

פַּקֻּעֹת   colocynths (Koops); gourds (DCH) (2 Kgs 4:39 H)

פִּשְׁתָּה   flax (for linen, wicks); wick of a lamp, made of flax (כְּלִי) (Exod 9:31 R)

צֶאֱלִים lotus plants (SDBH) (Job 40:21 R)

רֹאשׁ hemlock, poison; gall (Harrison) (Deut 29:17)

שׁוּשָׁן lily (Song 2:1)

Thorns, Thistles, Briars

אָטָד thorn-tree; bramble, thorn, thornbush (SDBH); boxthorn (Koops) (Judg 9:14 R)

חוֹחַ thorn; nose-ring (1 Sam 13:6)

חָרוּל weeds, nettles (SDBH) (Prov 24:31 R)

סִיר / סִירָה thorn; hook; pot (Eccl 7:6 R)

צְנִינִם thorn, pricks (Num 33:55 R)

קוֹץ thorn (Gen 3:18)

שָׁמִיר thorn; gem, diamond; briers (SDBH) (Isa 5:6 R)

Thistle/Briar

בַּרְקָנִים briars; threshing-sledges (Judg 8:7 R)

דַּרְדַּר thistle; thistles (DCH) (Hos 10:8 R)

שֵׂךְ briar; thorn (DCH) (Num 33:55 H)

Thicket/Hedge/Shrub

מְשׂוּכָה / מְסוּכָה hedge (thorns) (Prov 15:19 H)

נַעֲצוּץ thorny thicket; thorn, thistle, brier (SDBH) (Isa 7:19 R)

סְבַךְ thicket (SDBH) (Gen 22:13 R)

עָב thicket (SDBH) (Jer 4:29 H)

צֵן cactus hedge; barb (Job 5:5 R)

שַׂיִת wild growth, scrub (Isa 5:6 R)

Nettle/Prickle

חֵדֶק prickly plant; thorns; brier, nightshade (DCH) (Prov 15:19 R)

חָרוּל nettles (Koops) (Job 30:7 R)

סִלּוֹן prickle (Ezek 2:6 R)

סָרָבִים nettles (Koops) (Ezek 2:6 H)

סִרְפַּד nettle (Isa 55:13 H)

קִמּוֹשׂ prickly plant; weed, thistle, nettle (Prov 24:31 R)

שֵׂךְ prick (Koops); thorn (DCH) (Num 33:55 H)

Bushes and Shrubs

אֵזוֹב hyssop; marjoram (Koops) (Exod 12:22)

בְּדֹלַח bdellium (gum) (Gen 2:12 R)

כֹּפֶר henna (Song 4:13 R)

מַלּוּחַ mallow; sea-purslain (salt marsh plant) (Job 30:4 H)

מָן manna (Exod 16:15)

סְנֶה blackberry bush, bramble; generic word for bush, shrub (SDBH); burning bush (Koops) (Exod 3:2 R)

עַרְעָר/עֲרוֹעֵר juniper, tamarisk (DCH) (Jer 17:6 H)

רֹתֶם broom; broom tree (SDBH) (1 Kgs 19:4 R)

שְׁחֵלֶת onycha, used for incense (DCH) (Exod 30:34 H)

שִׂיחַ bush, plant, shrub, shoot (Gen 2:5 R)

Parts of Trees and Plants

Root

שֹׁרֶשׁ root (Job 14:8)

Stump

גֶּזַע trunk, stump (Isa 11:1 R)

Shoot

יְנִיקָה sucker, sapling (Ezek 17:4 H)

נֵצֶר shoot (Isa 11:1 R)

שֶׁלַח shoot (Song 4:13 R)

Sprout

יוֹנֶקֶת sprout (Ezek 17:22)

צֶמַח sprout (Hos 8:7)

Tendril

נְטִישָׁה tendril (Isa 18:5 R)

שָׂרִיג tendril, branch (Joel 1:7 R)

Twig

זַלְזַל twig; tremulous (Isa 18:5 H)

זָמִיר twig; pruning (DCH) (Song 2:12 H)

עָנָף twigs, branches, bow (Lev 23:40 R)

Branch

אָמִיר branch (of tree); summit (DCH) (Isa 17:6 R)

חֹטֶר branch, rod, twig (Isa 11:1 R)

כַּפָּה palm frond or leaf; branch of tree (DCH) (Lev 23:40 R)

מַטֶּה branch, tribe, rod (Isa 10:15)

סַנְסִנָּה palm branches, date tree stalk (Song 7:9 H)

סָעִיף branches, boughs; cleft, branch, crutch (בְּלִי) (Isa 2:21 R)

סְעַפָּה/סַרְעַפָּה branch (Ezek 31:8 R)

עָנֵף branching; full of branches (DCH) (Ezek 19:10 H)

שׂוֹבֶךְ interlaced boughs, thicket (2 Sam 18:9 H)

שׂוֹךְ branch (Judg 9:49 H)

שֶׁלַח branch; spear (Neh 4:17 R)

Bud/Bloom/Blossom

נִצָּה blossom (Gen 40:10 R)

נִצָּן blossom (Song 2:12 H)

סְמָדַר vine blossom (Song 2:13 R)

פְּטוּר opened bud (1 Kgs 6:18 R)

פֶּרַח bloom; bud, flower (DCH) (Isa 18:5)

Flower

נֵץ flower; kestrel (hawk) (Gen 40:10 H)

צִיץ flower; glistening (Isa 28:4)

Foliage/Leaf

דָּלִית foliage, branch, bough (Jer 11:16 R)

טָרָף leaf, fresh shoot (Gen 8:11 R)

עָבֹת foliage (Ezek 31:3 R)

עָלֶה leaf; foliage (Jer 17:8)

פֹּארָה foliage, bough, branch, shoot (Ezek 31:5 R)

צַמֶּרֶת foliage, top branch ("wool-like"); tree-top (DCH) (Ezek 31:3 R)

רַעֲנָן leafy, luxuriant (Deut 12:2)

Gardens and Planting Places

גַּן garden (Song 4:12)

גַּנָּה / גִנָּה garden (Isa 1:30)

גֹּרֶן threshing floor (Hos 9:2)

דַּיִשׁ threshing (Lev 26:5 H)

כֶּרֶם garden, vineyard (1 Kgs 21:1)

כַּרְמֶל planted field; orchard (DCH) (Isa 10:18)

מַטָּע place of planting; act/thing planted (Ezek 17:7 R)

מִקְשָׁה cucumber field; muskmellon, cantalope (Koops) (Jer 10:5 R)

עֲרוּגָה garden (Song 5:13 R)

פַּרְדֵּס park; orchard, forest (DCH) (Song 4:13 R)

שׂוּרָה row of plants in garden (SDBH) (Job 24:11 R)

PART II

THE HUMAN ORDER

HUMAN

General Terms

אָדָם   man, human; human, humankind (SDBH) (Gen 1:26)

אֱנוֹשׁ   man, mortal (Deut 32:26)

יָתוֹם   orphan (Parker), fatherless (SDBH) (Job 24:9)

נֶפֶשׁ   self, life, person; throat (Jer 31:12)

עִי   a ruined person (SDBH) (Job 30:24 R)

שְׁאֵר   male kindred, flesh (Lev 18:12)

שַׁאֲרָה   female kindred (Lev 18:17)

Male and Female

Male

אִישׁ   man, individual, husband; ages 25–60 (Eng) (Exod 1:1)

גֶּבֶר   adult man, ages 25–60 (Eng) (Jer 31:22)

זָכָר   male (Gen 17:14)

זָקֵן   leading citizen; elder (Ezek 27:9)

מַת   adult, man (Deut 33:6)

Female

אִשָּׁה   woman, wife (Gen 2:22)

בַּעֲלָה   lady, mistress of a house (DCH) (1 Kgs 17:17 R)

נְקֵבָה   female (Num 5:3)

שָׂרָה   noblewoman, princess (Isa 49:23 R)

Infant

בְּכוֹר   firstborn (Gen 36:15)

בְּכוֹרָה   birthright

גָּמוּל   weaned child (Isa 11:8)

גמל   to wean (Parker) (Gen 21:8)

טַף   little one, child; dependent, vulnerable (Parker) (Deut 1:39)

יוֹנֵק   infant, suckling (Lam 2:11 R)

ינק   to suck (a mother's breast) (Parker) (Exod 2:9)

עֲוִיל   child, infant (Job 19:18 R)

עוּל   infant, sucking, child (Isa 49:15 R)

עוֹלֵל   child, infant, little one; small child, in a situation of danger (Parker) (1 Sam 22:19)

פְּטֶר/פִּטְרָה   firstborn (Num 8:16 H)

שִׁלְיָה   fetus, afterbirth (Deut 28:57 H)

Youth

General

בְּחוּרוֹת / בְּחוּרִים period of youth nearing adulthood (Parker) (Eccl 11:9 R)

יַלְדָּה / יֶלֶד lad, offspring, child/girl; ages 0–3 years (Eng) (Exod 1:17)

נְעוּרִים youth, childhood (Parker) (Gen 46:34)

עֶלֶם adolescent; young man (DCH) (1 Sam 17:56)

עֲלוּמִים period of older youth (Parker) (Isa 54:4)

צְעִירָה young childhood (Parker) (Gen 43:33 R)

Male Youth

בָּחוּר young man, warrior (Deut 32:25)

וָלָד boy; child, fetus (DCH) (Gen 11:30 H)

יַלְדוּת boyhood (Eccl 11:9 R)

נַעַר boy, servant, retainer; ages 3–25 years (Eng) (Gen 21:12)

נֹעַר boyhood (Job 36:14 R)

נַעַר קָטֹן young boy, ages 3–13 years (Eng) (1 Kgs 3:7)

עֶלֶם male youth (Parker) (1 Sam 17:56 R)

Female Youth

בְּתוּלָה young woman, connotation of sexual maturity (Parker) (Deut 32:25)

בְּתוּלִים virginity (SDBH); young womanhood (DCH) (Lev 21:13)

יַלְדָּה young girl (Parker) (Gen 34:4 R)

נַעֲרָה girl (Gen 24:14)

עַלְמָה sexually mature female youth (Parker) (Isa 7:14 R)

Old Age

בָּאִים בַּיָּמִים advanced in years after a full life, ages 70+ (Eng) (Gen 18:11)

זָקֵן old age (Gen 48:10 H)

זָקֵן old; ages 60+ (Eng) (Judg 19:16)

זָקֵן מְאֹד advanced old age, ages 70+ (Eng) (1 Sam 2:22)

זִקְנָה old age (1 Kgs 11:4 R)

זְקֻנִים son born in old age (Gen 44:20 R)

יָשִׁישׁ old man; aged (SDBH) (Job 12:12 R)

שֵׂיבָה old age, gray hair, hoary head (Hos 7:9)

שֵׂיבָה טוֹבָה advanced old age, ages 70+ (Eng) (Gen 15:15)

Friend

(For Enemy, see Military ➡ Enemy)

אַלּוּף friend, familiar; chieftain (Ps 55:14)

חָבֵר fellow, friend, partner (SDBH) (Judg 20:11)

יָדִיד loved one, dear one, special friend (SDBH) (Deut 33:12 R)

כְּנָת colleague; associate (SDBH) (Ezra 4:7 H)

מֹדָע/מוֹדַע acquaintance (Ruth 2:1 R)

מַכָּר acquaintance (SDBH) (2 Kgs 12:6 R)

עָמִית comrade, kindred (Lev 25:15)

רֵעַ friend, associate (Job 30:29)

רֵעֶה companion (2 Sam 15:37 R)

רֵעָה female associate (Judg 11:37 R)

רְעוּת female associate (Exod 11:2 R)

רַעְיָה female associate (Judg 11:37)

Slaves/Servants

אָדוֹן slavemaster, lord (Bridge) (Gen 44:8)

אָמָה maidservant, female slave (Exod 20:10)

יְלִיד slave born in the house; one who is born (DCH) (Gen 14:14)

עֶבֶד male slave; slave, servant, officer, official, subject, vassal (SDBH) (Gen 14:15)

פִּילֶגֶשׁ concubine (Gen 22:24)

שָׂכִיר hireling, day-laborer (Exod 12:45)

שִׁפְחָה female slave (Gen 33:1)

Nations, Peoples

אֲגֻדָּה group, band (SDBH) (2 Sam 2:25 R)

אֶזְרָח citizen, native (Exod 12:19)

אֶלֶף clan (SDBH) (Num 1:16)

אֻמָּה community; tribe, people (SDBH) (Gen 25:16 R)

אָמוֹן throng (Jer 52:15 H)

אֲסַפְסֻף group of foreigners, connotation of "riffraff" or "rabble" (SDBH) (Num 11:4 H)

גּוֹי foreign nation (Gen 35:11)

גֵּר guest, foreigner (Gen 15:13)

דּוֹר generation (SDBH) (Gen 6:9)

זָר foreigner (Exod 29:33)

לְאֹם community, people, nation (Isa 51:4)

מַטֶּה tribe (SDBH) (Exod 31:2)

מַלְכֻת kingdom (Hurvitz) (Num 24:7)

מַקְהֵל assembly (SDBH) (Ps 26:12 R)

נָכְרִי foreigner (Judg 19:12)

עַם people, nation, army (Gen 11:6)

עֵרֶב/עֶרֶב mixed people; mixed rabble, foreigners (SDBH) (Exod 12:38 R)

שֵׁבֶט/שַׁרְבִיט tribe (SDBH) (Gen 49:16)

תּוֹשָׁב resident alien (Exod 12:45)

HUMAN ANATOMY

Head

גֹּבַח/גַּבַּחַת   bald forehead, receding hairline (Lev 13:55 R)

גֻּלְגֹּלֶת   skull, head (Judg 9:53)

מֵצַח   forehead, brow (Isa 48:4)

פֵּאָה   hairline; corner (Lev 13:41)

פְּאַת רֹאשׁ   temple (Hobbins) (Lev 19:27 H)

פַּת/פֵּאָה/פַּאֲתַיִם   temple (Hobbins) (Isa 3:17 R)

קָדְקֹד   crown of head, pate (Deut 28:35)

קֵרֵחַ/קָרַחַת/קָרְחָה   bald spot (back of head) (Jer 47:5)

רֹאשׁ   head (Hobbins) (Gen 48:14)

רַקָּה   temple of head (Hobbins) (Song 4:3 R)

Hair

גִּזְרָה   coiffure (Lam 4:7 R)

דַּלָּה   hair (DCH); tresses (Hobbins) (Song 7:6 R)

זָקָן   beard (Hobbins) (Lev 13:29)

פְּאַת זָקָן   sidegrowth of beard (Lev 19:27 R)

פֶּרַע   long hair (Judg 5:2 R)

צִיצִת   lock of hair, tassel (Num 15:38 R)

קְוֻצּוֹת   locks (Hobbins) (Song 5:2 R)

שֵׂיבָה   gray hair, hoary; old age (Hos 7:9)

שֵׂעָר   hair (Lev 13:3)

שָׂפָם   moustache (2 Sam 19:24 R)

Face

אֹזֶן/אוֹזֶן/אָזְנַיִם   ear (Exod 29:20)

אָחוֹר   back of head (Hobbins) (Ezek 8:16)

אִישׁוֹן   pupil (Deut 32:10 R)

אַף   nostril, nose (Amos 4:10)

בָּבָה   pupil (Zech 2:12 H)

בְּדַל-אֹזֶן   earlobe (Amos 3:12)

גַּב   brow, eyebrow (Lev 14:9)

דַּל שְׂפָתַיִם   door of the lips (poetic) (Hobbins) (Ps 141:3 H)

דִּמְעָה   tears (SDBH) (2 Kgs 20:5)

חֵךְ   palate (Ps 119:103)

לְחִי/לְחָיַיִם   jaw-bone, cheek (Judg 15:15)

לָשׁוֹן   tongue, language (Exod 4:10)

מִדְבָּר   mouth (poetic) (Hobbins) (Song 4:3 H)

מַלְקוֹחַיִם   jaws (Ps 22:16 H)

מְתַלְעוֹת/מַלְתְּעוֹת   tooth, biter, molar (Joel 1:6 R)

עַיִן/עֵינַיִם   eye (Gen 46:4)

עַפְעַפַּיִם   eyelash; eyelids (Hobbins) (Prov 4:25)

פְּאַת פָּנִים   corner or side of the face, temple (Hobbins) (Lev 13:41 R)

פֶּה   mouth (Neh 9:20)

פָּנִים   face (Lev 13:41)

שְׁמֻרוֹת עֵינַיִם   eyelids (Hobbins) (Ps 77:5 H)

שֵׁן   tooth (Deut 19:21)

שָׂפָה/שְׂפָתַיִם   lip, language; edge, brink, shore (Exod 6:12)

תְּנוּךְ   earlobe (Exod 29:20 R)

Neck

גַּרְגְּרוֹת   neck, outside of neck (Prov 1:9 R)

מַפְרֶקֶת   vertebra of neck (1 Sam 4:18 H)

עֹרֶף   back of neck; nape of neck (Hobbins) (Isa 48:4)

צַוָּאר   neck, back of neck (Gen 27:40)

Throat

גָּרוֹן   throat; windpipe (Ps 5:10 R)

לֹעַ   throat, gullet (Prov 23:2 H)

נֶפֶשׁ   throat; self (Prov 3:22)

Upper Body

דַּד   breast (Prov 5:19 R)

דַּד   nipples (Hobbins) (Ezek 23:3 R)

דָּם   blood (Gen 9:4)

זִיז   teat (Hobbins) (Isa 66:11 H)

זֵעָה   perspiration, sweat (SDBH) (Gen 3:19 H)

חָזֶה   chest (Lev 7:31)

כָּתֵף   shoulder (Num 7:9)

לֵב/לֵבָב   heart; "mind" (Isa 40:2)

נֶפֶשׁ   life-breath (Hobbins) (Gen 35:18)

נֵצַח   juice, blood (Hobbins) (Isa 63:3 R)

נְשָׁמָה   breath (Wilkinson) (Gen 2:7)

סְגוֹר לֵב   pericardium, membrane enclosing the heart (Hos 13:8 H)

רוּחַ   air (Hobbins) (Exod 15:8)

שַׁד/שָׁדַיִם   breast; (female) breast (DCH) (Ezek 16:7)

Arm/Hand

אֶצְבַּע   finger, toe (Exod 29:12)

אַצִּיל   knuckle; joint (Jer 38:12 R)

אַצִּילוֹת יָד   armpits (Hobbins) (Jer 38:12 H)

אַצִּילֵי יָד   elbows (Hobbins) (Ezek 13:18 H)

בֹּהֶן   thumb; big toe (Judg 1:6)

זְרוֹעַ   arm (2 Sam 1:10)

חֹפֶן   hollow (of hand) (Ezek 10:2 R)

יָד / יָדַיִם   hand; penis (euphemism) (Gen 3:22)

שְׂמֹאל   left hand (Hobbins) (Song 2:6)

כַּף   palm (of hand); sole (of foot) (1 Sam 5:4)

יָמִין   right hand (Hobbins) (Gen 48:13)

צִפֹּרֶן   fingernail (Deut 21:12 R)

קֹטֶן   little finger; little one, in reference to finger or penis (DCH) (1 Kgs 12:10 R)

קָנֶה   humerus bone (Hobbins) (Job 31:22)

שְׁעָלִים   hollows of hands (Isa 40:12 R)

Bones

גֶּרֶם   bone, self; bone, strength (DCH) (Gen 49:14 R)

מֹחַ   bone marrow (Wilkinson) (Job 21:24 H)

עָצֶה   spine; sacrum (DCH) (Lev 3:9 H)

עֶצֶם   bone, self (Lam 4:7)

צֵלָע   spine; rib (Gen 2:22)

Abdomen

אוּל   paunch (Hobbins); belly (DCH) (Ps 73:4 H)

בֶּטֶן   belly, womb (Ps 31:9)

גָּחוֹן   belly, stomach, abdomen (Gen 3:14 R)

גֹּלֶם   embryo (Wilkinson) (Ps 139:16 H)

חַדְרֵי־בָטֶן   "inner room of the abdomen" (Wilkinson); innards of body (DCH) (Prov 18:8 R)

חֵיק   lap, bosom (Exod 4:6)

חֹמֶשׁ   stomach (Hobbins) (2 Sam 2:23 R)

טַבּוּר   navel (Judg 9:37 R)

כָּרֵשׂ   belly; stomach (Hobbins) (Jer 51:34 H)

מֵעָה / מֵעִים   abdomen, intestines (2 Sam 20:10)

מַשְׁבֵּר   orifice of womb; mouth of the womb (Hobbins); mouth of cervix (DCH) (Hos 13:13 H)

קֵבָה   belly (Hobbins) (Deut 18:3 R)

קִיא   to vomit, to throw up (SDBH) (Jer 25:27 R)

קֶרֶב   entrails, bowels, heart, mind; inward parts (Hobbins); trunk of body (Wilkinson) (Exod 29:17)

רֶחֶם   womb, belly (Jer 20:17)

שֹׁר   navel, umbilical cord; vulva (Wilkinson) (Song 7:3 R)

Kidney/Liver

טְחוֹת   inward parts, kidneys (Job 38:36 R)

כָּבֵד   liver (Lam 2:11 H)

כִּלְיָה   kidney; "conscience" (Ps 139:13)

מְרֹרָה   gall bladder (Hobbins); bile or gall (Wilkinson) (Job 20:14 R)

Loins

חֲלָצַיִם   loins (Job 31:20)

כֶּסֶל / כְּסָלִים   loins (Hobbins); thighs (DCH) (Ps 38:8 R)

מָתְנַיִם   hips, loins (Exod 12:11)

Back

בָּמוֹת   back (Hobbins) (Isa 2:22 R)

גַּב   back (Ps 129:3)

גֵּו / גֵּו / גֵּוָה   back, self (Ezek 40:13 R)

שְׁכֶם / שִׁכְמָה   back (Hobbins); shoulder (DCH) (Exod 12:34)

Buttocks/Hip/Anus

כַּף הַיָּרֵךְ   hip-socket (Hobbins) (Gen 32:33 H)

מִפְשָׂעָה   buttocks, hip (1 Chr 19:4 H)

נָשֶׁה   sciatic nerve (Hobbins) (Gen 32:33 H)

קֵבָה   anus; vulva; abdomen (Num 25:8 H)

שֵׁתָה / שָׁתוֹת / שֵׁת   buttocks (2 Sam 10:4 R)

Excrement

דֹּמֶן   dung (SDBH) (2 Kgs 9:37 R)

חֲרָאִים   dung, excrement (SDBH) (2 Kgs 6:25 R)

מַדְמֵנָה   dung-pit (DCH) (Isa 25:10 H)

פֶּרֶשׁ   dung, offal (SDBH); intestines, excrement (DCH) (Exod 29:14 R)

צֵאָה / צֹאָה   excrement, dung (SDBH) (Deut 23:14 R)

מֵימֵי רַגְלַ   urine, literally "penis water" (Wilkinson) (Isa 36:12)

שַׁיִן   urine (SDBH) (2 Kgs 18:27 R)

Genitals

General

יָרֵךְ   vulva (Wilkinson) (Song 7:2)

כֶּסֶל / כְּסָלִים   loins, genitalia (Hobbins) (Lev 3:4 R)

עֶרְוָה   genitals (male, female); nakedness (Gen 9:22)

Male

אֶשֶׁךְ	testicle (Lev 21:20 H)
בָּשָׂר	flesh, penis (Hobbins) (Exod 28:42)
זִרְמָה	phallus, semen; emission of sperm (SDBH) (Ezek 23:20 R)
חֲלָצַיִם	testicles (Boer) (Gen 35:11 R)
יָד / יָדַיִם	penis (euphemism); hand (Jer 5:31)
יָרֵךְ	male genitals (Gen 24:2), vagina (Boer)
מְבוּשִׁים	male genitals (Gen 24:2), vagina (Boer)
מָבֻשׁ	male genitals (Deut 25:11 H)
מַקֵּל	staff, club, penis (DCH) (Hos 4:12)
מַשְׁכִּים	testicles (Boer) (Jer 5:8 H)
מָתְנַיִם	testicles (Boer) (Job 40:16 R)
עָרְלָה	foreskin (Deut 10:16)
פַּחַד	testicle (Job 40:17 H)
קֹטֶן	little finger; little one, in reference to finger or penis (DCH) (1 Kgs 12:10 R)
רֶגֶל / רַגְלַיִם	penis, genitals (euphemism); leg, foot (Judg 3:24)
שָׁפְכָה	penis, urethra (Deut 23:2 H)

Female

בְּשַׂר עֶרְוָה	flesh of nakedness, female genitalia (Lev 28:42 R)
דוה	to menstruate (SDBH) (Lev 12:2 H)
יָרֵךְ	vagina (Song 7:2), male genitals (Boer)
מְבוּשִׁים	shameful things, female genitalia (Hobbins); male genitalia (DCH) (Deut 25:11 H)
מַעַר	nakedness, female genitalia (Hobbins) (Nah 3:5 R)
נַבְלוּת	shamelessness, female genitalia (Hobbins) (Hos 2:12 H)
עֶרְוָה	nakedness, female genitalia (Hobbins) (Gen 9:22)
שׁוּחָה	possibly vagina (DCH); gorge, pits; pit (SDBH) (Prov 23:27 R)
שֹׁר	navel, umbilical cord; vulva (Wilkinson) (Song 7:3 R)

———————————————— Leg ————————————————

בֶּרֶךְ / בִּרְכַּיִם	knee (1 Kgs 19:18)
יָרֵךְ / יְרֵכִים	thigh (Num 5:21)
כְּרָע	lower leg (below knee) (Exod 12:9 R)
מַרְגְּלוֹת	legs (Hobbins); place of feet (DCH) (Ruth 3:4 R)
עָטִין	thigh (Hobbins) (Job 21:24 H)
רֶגֶל / רַגְלַיִם	leg, foot; penis, genitals (euphemism) (Ezek 25:6)
שׁוֹק	leg, calf (Lev 7:33)

Foot

אֲפָסַיִם	ankles (Hobbins) (Ezek 47:3 H)
אֶצְבַּע	finger, toe (1 Chr 20:6)
בֹּהֶן	big toe, thumb (Lev 8:23)
יָחֵף	barefoot (2 Sam 15:30 R)
כַּף / כַּפַּיִם	palm (of hand); sole (of foot) (Deut 2:5)
עָקֵב	heel (Gen 3:15)
פַּעַם	foot (Hobbins) (Ps 17:5)
קַרְסֹל	ankle (2 Sam 22:37 R)
רֶגֶל / רַגְלַיִם	foot, feet (Hobbins) (Ezek 25:6)

Body/Muscle

בָּשָׂר	flesh, body; person; skin (Wilkinson) (Isa 10:18)
גְּוִיָּה	body (Gen 47:18)
גּוּפָה	body (Hobbins) (1 Chr 10:12)
גִּיד	tendon; sinew (Hobbins) (Job 40:17 R)
גֶּלֶד	skin (Hobbins) (Job 16:15 H)
גַּף	body; self; back (Exod 21:3 R)
לְחוּם	flesh, body (Zeph 1:17 R)
עוֹר	skin (Hobbins) (Exod 22:26)
עֹצֶם	frame of body (Hobbins) (Ps 139:15 H)
צַד	side (Hobbins) (Num 33:55)
קַעֲקַע	tattoo (Lev 19:28 H)
שְׁאֵר	flesh, self (Lev 18:12)
שָׁרִיר	muscle, sinew (Job 40:16 H)

Body Fat

חֵלֶב	fat (Hobbins) (Judg 3:22)
מִשְׁמָן	fat (Hobbins) (Ps 78:31 R)
פִּימָה	fat (Hobbins) (Job 15:27 H)

Corpse

גּוּפָה	corpse (1 Chr 10:12 R)
נְבֵלָה	corpse, carcass (Ps 79:2)
פֶּגֶר	corpse, carcass (1 Sam 17:46)

DISEASE, MORTALITY, AND DISABILITY

Disease

חָלְאָה   disease; rust (Ezek 24:6 R)

חֳלִי   disease, malady, sickness (Jer 10:19)

מָזֶה   sickness; emaciated, thin (DCH) (Deut 32:24 H)

מַחֲלָה   sickness, infirmity (1 Kgs 8:37 R)

מַחֲלֶה   disease, sickness, suffering (pl.) (Prov 18:14 R)

נֶגֶף   affliction, plague (Exod 12:13 R)

צָרֶבֶת   scab, scar, burning; inflammation (DCH) (Lev 13:23 R)

קֶטֶב   pestilence; plague; deadly disease; destruction (SDBH) (Deut 32:24 R)

Specific Diseases

גָּרָב   eczema (DCH) (Lev 21:20 R)

יַבֶּלֶת   wen, seeping sore (Stewart); running sore, perhaps wart (DCH) (Lev 22:22 H)

יַלֶּפֶת   tetter, eczema, impetigo (Stewart); scab (DCH) (Lev 21:20 R)

עֹפֶל   "plague with swellings" (Kottek); hemorrhoid (DCH) (1 Sam 5:6 R)

צָרַעַת   collective term for skin diseases (Grzybowski and Nita); possibilities include eczema or psoriasis, ringworm, scabies, boils, burns (Williams) (Lev 13:2)

קַדַּחַת   inflammation, fever (Lev 26:16 R)

שַׁחֶפֶת   consumption (SDBH); illness (DCH) (Lev 26:16 R)

Medical Tools, Herbs

General

אָבְנָיִם   birthstool (Pritz); pair of stones (used as birthstool) (DCH) (Exod 1:16)

אֲפֵר   bandage (Pritz) (1 Kgs 20:38 R)

חִתּוּל   bandage (Pritz) (Ezek 30:21 H)

מָזוֹר   wound, bandage (Hos 5:13 R)

מְכֵרָה   circumcision blade (DCH) (Gen 49:5 H)

תְּעָלָה   bandage, plaster; water channel (Jer 30:13 R)

Herbs

אֲהָלוֹת/אֲהָלִים   aloes, agarwood; used as purgative (Harrison); used to treat burns and abrasions on skin (Koops) (Num 24:6 R)

אֵזוֹב   hyssop; marjoram (Koops); used for digestion and healing animal bites and scratches (Harrison) (Exod 12:22)

בָּצָל   onion; used to treat wounds (Williams) (Num 11:5 H)

בְּשָׂם/בֶּשֶׂם/בֹּשֶׂם balsam, spices; general term for aromatic spices, balms (Nielsen) (Song 5:13)

גַּד coriander; used to aid digestion (Harrison) (Exod 16:31 R)

דְּבֶלֶת תְּאֵנִים fig cake, used to heal skin wounds (Pritz) (2 Kgs 20:7)

דּוּדָאִים mandrake, love apple (SDBH); narcotic, used to aid infertility (Harrison, Williams) (Gen 30:14–16 R)

הֲדַס myrtle; crushed leaves used for skin health (Harrison); also used to treat gum disease and internal ulcers (Williams) (Neh 8:15 R)

זַיִת olive; olive tree, olive grove; olive oil used to treat cuts and wounds (Harrison, Williams) (Exod 23:11)

חֶלְבְּנָה galbanum (resin gum), fennel; used as deodorant (Harrison); milky or white substance (Nielsen) (Exod 30:34 H)

כַּמֹּן cummin; used to relieve gas and aid digestion (Harrison); used to treat sore throats and possibly also respiratory problems (Williams) (Isa 28:25 R)

כֻּסֶּמֶת fitches, spelt (Harrison); used to relieve gas and aid digestion (Harrison) (Ezek 4:9 R)

כַּרְכֹּם saffron; deodorant and digestive aid (Harrison) (Song 4:14 H)

לֹט ladanum (SDBH); used for coughs and dysentery (Koops) (Gen 37:25 R)

לַעֲנָה wormwood; used to kill internal parasites and as expectorant (Harrison) (Deut 29:17 R)

שְׁחֵלֶת onycha, used to make incense (DCH) (Exod 30:34 H)

מֹר myrrh; used to relieve flatulence (Harrison) (Exod 30:23)

מָרֹר bitter herbs (Exod 12:8 R)

נָטָף stacte resin; used to relieve coughs and stimulate menstruation (Harrison); storax, balm (Nielsen) (Exod 30:34 H)

נְכֹאת gum tragacanth (Koops); ladanum (CDC) (Gen 37:25 R)

נֵרְדְּ nard, spikenard (amber-colored oil) (Song 1:12 R)

עֲרָבִים poplar; willow (pl. only); used as natural aspirin (Williams) (Ps 137:2 R)

פְּקָעִים gourds (pl.); gourd-shaped ornament (DCH); used to make castor oil, a laxative (Harrison) (1 Kgs 6:18 R)

צֳרִי storax; balm (SDBH) (Gen 37:25 R)

קִדָּה cassia bark (aromatic); used as aphrodisiac, to aid digestion, and to stimulate blood flow to a part of the body (Harrison) (Exod 30:24 R)

קִיקָיוֹן castor-oil tree; gourd (Harrison); used to make castor oil, a laxative (Harrison, Koops) (Jonah 4:6 R)

קָנֶה calamus reed (Harrison); sweet cane, ginger grass (Koops); unclear use (Harrison) (Ezek 27:19)

קֶצַח nutmeg (black cummin); fitches, spelt, used to relieve gas and aid digestion (Harrison); nigella (Koops); black cumin (DCH) (Isa 28:25 R)

רִמּוֹן pomegranate; pomegranate fruit, pomegranate tree (DCH); used to eradicate intestinal worms (Williams) (Exod 28:33)

שׁוּם garlic; used to expel parasites and heal abcesses (Williams) (Num 11:5 H)

שֶׁמֶן oil, ointment (Pritz) (Isa 1:6)

תְּאֵנָה fig; fig tree (SDBH); used to treat boils (Williams) (2 Kgs 20:7)

תֹּמֶר/תִּמֹרָה/תָּמָר date-palm; possibly used to treat epilepsy, ear infections, coughs (Williams) (Exod 15:27)

Wound

חַבּוּרָה wound, bruise (Isa 1:6 R)

מַדְקָרָה piercing, stab (Prov 12:18 H)

מָזוֹר wound, bandage (Hos 5:13 R)

מַכָּה wound, blow, slaughter; stroke, blow stripe (DCH) (Prov 20:30)

נָכֵא stricken, wounded (Prov 17:22 R)

פֶּצַע wound, bruise (Isa 1:6 R)

תְּעָלָה bandage, plaster; water channel (Jer 30:13 R)

Pain

חַלְחָלָה writhing, terror, trembling (Ezek 30:4 R)

חַרְצֹב pangs, grief; bands (Ps 73:4)

כְּאֵב pain, anguish (Job 2:13 R)

כָּפָן hunger (Job 5:22 R)

עִצָּבוֹן pain, labor, toil (Gen 3:16 R)

עַצֶּבֶת pain, injury (Ps 16:4 R)

Disabilities

Physical

אִלֵּם unable to speak, "mute" (Olyan) (Isa 35:6 R)

גִּבֵּן curvature of back (Lev 21:20 H)

חָרֻם mutilated, disfigured; flat nose (?) (Lev 21:18)

חֵרֵשׁ hearing impaired, deaf (Isa 42:18 R)

מוּם blemish, defect (Olyan) (Deut 15:21)

מָעוֹג unable to walk, lame person (DCH) (Ps 35:16 H)

עִוֵּר visually impaired, blind (Isa 42:18)

פִּסֵּחַ physically impaired, limp, limping (2 Sam 9:13)

צֹלֵעָה someone with a limp, limper (Olyan) (Zeph 3:19 R)

קָלוּט stunted limb, short stature (Lev 22:23 H)

שָׂרוּעַ stretched, extended; big ear (?) (Lev 21:18 R)

תְּבַלֻּל eye-cataract (Lev 21:20 H)

תָּמִים unblemished, faultless, perfect (Stewart) (Song 5:2)

Mental Illness

מְשֻׁגָּע usually translated "crazy person," but possibly mentally ill (Olyan) (2 Kgs 9:11 R)

שִׁגָּעוֹן madness, mental illness (Olyan) (Deut 28:28 R)

Sexual/Reproductive Dysfunction

זָב genital flow (Olyan), genital discharges (Stewart) (Num 5:2)

כְּרוּת שָׁפְכָה castrated penis (Stewart) (Deut 23:2)

מְרוֹחַ אָשֶׁךְ crushed testicles (Stewart) (Lev 21:20)

עָקָר / עֲקָרָה infertile, barren person (Stewart) (Deut 7:14)

פְּצוּעַ־דַּכָּא crushed testicles (Stewart) (Deut 23:2)

רֶחֶם מַשְׁכִּיל miscarrying womb (Stewart) (Hos 9:14)

Death, Burial, Mourning

Death

אָבַד destruction (SDBH) (Num 24:20 R)

אַבְדָן / אָבְדָן destruction; extermination (SDBH) (Esth 9:5 R)

חָלָל slain (Num 19:18)

טֶבַח / טִבְחָה slaughter (of animal) (SDBH) (Ps 44:23)

טֶרֶף / טְרֵפָה prey; victim (SDBH) (Gen 31:39)

מָוֶת death (Gen 25:11)

מַחֲנָק strangling (SDBH) (Job 7:15 H)

מַפַּח breathing one's last (SDBH) (Job 11:20 H)

רְפָאִים dead spirits, ghosts (Prov 21:16 R)

שַׁחַת pit, destruction (Ps 55:24)

Burial

אָרוֹן coffin (Pritz) (Gen 50:26 H)

גָּדִישׁ burial heap; pile of sheaves (Job 21:32 R)

מִטָּה bier, coffin (Pritz) (2 Sam 3:31 H)

מְסַפֵּר embalmer, anointer (Amos 6:10 H)

צַלְמָוֶת grave, death; shadow (Amos 5:8)

צְרִיחַ tomb, grave (Pritz) (1 Sam 13:6 H)

קְבוּרָה sepulcher, grave (Gen 35:20)

קֶבֶר grave, tomb, burial (Gen 23:4)

בֵּית קְבָרוֹת burial site (Hurvitz) (Neh 2:3)

שְׁאוֹל underworld, sheol, grave (Gen 37:35)

Mourning

אֵבֶל lamentation; mourning, lamenting; mourner, lamenter (DCH) (Gen 37:35 R)

אֲנָחָה sighing, groaning (Ps 38:10)

אֲנִיָּה groaning (Lam 2:5 R)

בִּגְדֵי־אֵבֶל mourning clothes (Pritz) (2 Sam 14:2)

בְּכִית weeping (Gen 50:4)

מִסְפֵּד wailing, lamentation, mourning (Gen 50:10)

שַׂק sackcloth, mourning clothes (Pritz) (Gen 37:34 R)

FOOD AND SPICES
Food/Drink: General Terms

General

אֲכִילָה   food, meal, meat (1 Kgs 19:8 H)

אֹכֶל   food (Ps 104:21)

אָכְלָה   food (Ezek 15:4)

אֲרֻחָה   food, ration (2 Kgs 25:30 R)

בָּרוּת   food, meat (Ps 69:22 H)

בִּרְיָה   food, meat, meal (2 Sam 13:10 R)

טֶרֶף   food (SDBH); prey of beasts, food for humans (DCH) (Num 23:24)

יְבוּל   yield of soil, produce; crops, produce (SDBH) (Hab 3:17)

לֶחֶם   food, bread, grain (Lev 23:17)

מַאֲכָל   food (Gen 2:9)

מָזוֹן   food, meat (2 Chr 11:23 R)

מַכֹּלֶת   food (1 Kgs 5:25 H)

מָן   manna, connected with Tamarix mannifera (UBS) (Exod 16:15)

מָנָה   portion (Esth 2:9)

מַטְעָם   morsel, food, delicacy (Prov 23:3 R)

מַרְזֵחַ   banquet (Walsh); feasting, funeral meal (DCH) (Jer 16:5 R)

מִשְׁתֶּה   banquet (Walsh); feast, drink (DCH) (Esth 1:3)

נָזִיד   stew (FAJ) (Gen 25:29 R)

פַּנַּג   unknown baked food (Borowski *Agriculture*); millet (Koops); early figs, pastry, millet, or pancakes or opopanax (DCH) (Ezek 27:17 H)

צֵידָה   food, game; provision of food (DCH) (Gen 27:3)

תָּפֵל   tasteless, insipid food (SDBH) (Job 6:6 R)

Animal Fodder

בְּלִיל   fodder, food for animals (SDBH) (Isa 30:24 R)

מִסְפּוֹא   fodder, food for animals (SDBH, Koops) (Gen 24:25 R)

Drink

מַיִם   water (Gen 21:14)

מִשְׁתֶּה   banquet (Walsh); feast, drink (DCH) (Esth 1:3)

עָסִיס   juice (Brenner "The Food of Love"); sweet wine, juice (DCH); must, fresh wine (SDBH) (Joel 1:5 R)

שִׁקּוּי   beverage, possibly wine (Jordan) (Hos 2:7 R)

Taste

טוֹב sweet, tasty (Brenner "The Food of Love") (Song 1:2)

מָתוֹק sweet (Brenner "The Food of Love"); sweet, sweet thing, sweetness (DCH) (Prov 24:13)

Grains

אָבִיב ripe ears of corn; newly formed ears of grain (Koops); ear of cereal (DCH) (Lev 2:14 R)

אֵיפָה grain measure (40 liters) (Exod 16:36)

בִּכּוּרִים firstfruits (of fruits and grain) (Ezek 44:30)

בְּלִיל fodder, food for animals (SDBH) (Isa 30:24 R)

בַּר grain (Prov 14:4)

גָּדִישׁ sheaves (Koops); shock of grain (DCH) (Job 5:26 R)

גֶּרֶשׂ crushed grains, grits (Lev 2:14 R)

דָּגָן grain; cereal (Borowski *Agriculture*); corn, grain of cereals (DCH) (Ps 4:8)

דֹּחַן millet, sorghum (Ezek 4:9 H)

זֶרַע sowing, seed, grain (Koops) (Gen 47:19)

חִטָּה wheat (1 Kgs 5:25)

יֵרָקוֹן mildew (Koops); rust or mildew (DCH) (1 Kgs 8:37 R)

כֻּסֶּמֶת spelt; spelt, emmer (SDBH); wheat (Koops); emmer wheat (MacDonald); spelt (DCH) (Ezek 4:9 R)

כַּרְמֶל new grain; fruit, growth; raw grain (Borowski *Agriculture*); fresh ears of grain (Koops); fresh ears (of cereal) (DCH) (2 Kgs 4:42 R)

מְלִילוֹת ear of grain (Borowski *Agriculture*); ear of corn (DCH) (Deut 23:26 H)

נִסְמָן sesame (?), millet (?) (Borowski *Agriculture*); "the thing planted" (DCH) (Isa 28:25 H)

סֹלֶת fine flour; semolina, choice wheat or flour (DCH) (Gen 18:6)

עֲבוּר produce, grain (Koops) (Josh 5:11–12 R)

עָמִיר cut grain, sheaves (SDBH) (Jer 9:21 R)

פִּשְׁתָּה flax (Borowski *Agriculture*) (Exod 9:31 R)

קָלִי roasted grain, parched grain; roasted, dried, or baked kernels of grain (Koops); roasted grain, parched grain, or perhaps roasted lentils (DCH) (Lev 23:14 R)

קָמָה ripe, uncut grain plants (Koops); standing grain (DCH); standing grain (SDBH) (Isa 17:5)

קֶמַח flour, meal (Num 5:15)

קַשׁ chaff, straw; stubble, chaff (DCH) (Exod 15:7)

רִיפוֹת crushed grains (pl.); barley groats (DCH) (2 Sam 17:19 R)

שִׁבֹּלֶת ear of grain (Isa 17:5)

שְׂעֹרָה   barley (Lev 27:16)

תֶּבֶן   straw, grain stalks (Gen 24:25)

Threshing/Winnowing

גֹּרֶן   threshing floor (Hos 9:2)

דַּיִשׁ   threshing time; threshing (DCH) (Lev 26:5 H)

חָרוּץ   threshing sledge, incised, sharpened (Job 41:22 R)

חָרִיץ   sharpened; pickaxe (DCH) (2 Sam 12:31 R)

מוֹרַג   threshing sledge (2 Sam 24:22 R)

מִזְרֶה   winnowing shovel (fan, fork); pitchfork (DCH) (Jer 15:7 R)

רַחַת   winnowing fork; winnowing shovel (DCH) (Isa 30:24 H)

Grain: Baked Goods/Dough/Leaven

בָּצֵק   dough, flour (Exod 12:34 R)

לָשָׁד   cake; cake, delicacy (DCH) (Num 11:8 R)

חַלָּה   ring bread; cake (DCH) (Lev 24:5)

חָמֵץ   leavened bread (Lev 7:13)

חֹרִי   white bread (Gen 40:16 H)

כַּוָּן   cake (for idols), wafer (Jer 7:18 R)

לְבִבוֹת/לְבִיבַת   cakes (pl.); hearty dumplings (FAJ) (2 Sam 13:6 R)

לֶחֶם   bread, food; bread, bread grain, grain (Koops) (Lev 23:17)

מָעוֹג   cake, bread; loaf or slice of bread or cake (DCH); round silo (DCH) (1 Kgs 17:12 H)

מַצָּה   unleavened bread (Exod 12:39)

עֻגָה   cake (on hot stones) (Hos 7:8)

עֲרִיסָה   coarse meal, dough; wheat (Brenner "The Food of Love") (Ezek 44:30 R)

צָלִיל/צְלוּל   round loaf/cake (Judg 7:13 H)

רָקִיק   flat cakes; wafer (SDBH) (Lev 2:4 R)

שְׂאֹר   leaven (Exod 12:15 R)

Vine, Wine, Grapes (includes Strong Drink)

Plant Parts

גֶּפֶן   vine (2 Kgs 4:39)

זְמוֹרָה   twig; branch of vine (Isa 17:10 R)

נָזִיר   untrimmed vine (Lev 25:5 R)

שָׂרִיג   tendril; branch of vine (DCH) (Gen 40:10 R)

שֹׂרֵק/שֹׂרֵקָה   vinestock; choice vine (Walsh); variety of grape, choicest grape (Borowski *Agriculture*) (Isa 5:2 R)

Wine/Strong Drink

דַּם־עֲנָבִים / דַּם־עֵנָב   poetic phrase for wine, lit "blood of grape(s)"
(Borowski *Agriculture*) (Gen 49:11)

חֹמֶץ   vinegar (fermented grape plus barley); sour wine, vinegar
(SDBH) (Ruth 2:14 R)

חֶמֶר/חֲמַר   wine (root = boil); (fermenting) wine (SDBH); red (?) wine
(Borowski *Agriculture*) (Deut 32:14)

יַיִן   wine, wine-induced stupor (DCH) (Gen 9:24)

יֵין הָרֶקַח   spiced wine (Borowski *Agriculture*) (Song 8:2)

מֶזֶג   mixed wine = spiced; mixed wine (DCH) (Song 7:3 H)

מִמְסָךְ   mixed drink, spiced wine (Walsh); ritual wine, libation wine
(Jordan) (Prov 23:30 R)

מַמְתַקִּים   sweet wine (SDBH); sweetness, sweet things, perhaps
sweet drink (DCH); sweets (Brenner "The Food of Love")
(Song 5:16 R)

מֶסֶךְ   mixed drink, spiced wine (SDBH) (Ps 75:9 H)

מַשְׁקֶה   drink (Lev 11:34 R)

מִשְׁרָה   juice; syrup, a grape product forbidden to Nazirites, perhaps
equivalent to modern Arabic dibs (Borowski *Agriculture*);
juice (DCH) (Num 6:3 H)

סֹבֶא   drink, wine, liquor; alcoholic drink (Walsh); strong drink
(DCH); wine, possibly beer (Jordan) (Hos 4:18 R)

עָסִיס   new wine (Walsh); must, new wine (de Blois); pomegranate
wine (Borowski *Agriculture*); sweet wine, juice (DCH)
(Joel 1:5 R)

צוּף   honeycomb (SDBH); mead (Borowski *Daily Life*)
(Ps 19:11 R)

שֵׁכָר   liquor, strong drink; date-wine (SDBH); beer
(Borowski *Agriculture*); generic term for alcoholic drinks
(MacDonald); fermented drink (DCH) (Prov 20:1)

שֶׁמֶר   dregs; lees, dregs of wine, wine matured on the lees (DCH)
(Ps 75:9 R)

שִׁקּוּי   beverage, possibly wine (Jordan) (Hos 2:7 R)

תִּירוֹשׁ   new wine (Isa 65:8)

Cluster/Grape

אֲשִׁישָׁה   raisins (Brenner "The Food of Love"), raisin cake (DCH,
SDBH, Koops, MacDonald) (2 Sam 6:19 R)

אֶשְׁכּוֹל   cluster, bunch (Song 1:14 R)

בֹּסֶר   unripe grape (SDBH, Koops) (Isa 18:5 R)

בָּצִיר   grape harvest, vintage, clipped (Isa 24:13 R)

זָג   grapeskin, pit; skin or seed of grape (DCH) (Num 6:4 H)

חַרְצָן   unripe grape, pit, seeds; sour grape (DCH) (Num 6:4 H)

סְמָדַר   type of grape, usually translated "grape blossom"
(Borowski *Agriculture*); buds or blossoms of vine, perhaps
blossom-flavored wine (DCH) (Song 7:13 R)

עֹלֵלוֹת   grape gleanings (pl.) (Judg 8:2 R)

עֵנָב   grape (Hos 9:10)

פֶּרֶט   fallen grapes (Lev 19:10 H)

צִמּוּק   raisin cake; dried grapes, raisin cake (DCH); raisin
(Borowski *Agriculture*) (1 Sam 25:18 R)

Vineyard

גָּדֵר   vineyard walls (Walsh) (Isa 5:5)

גַּת   winepress, threshing floor (DCH); treading floor (Jordan)
(Isa 63:2 R)

כֶּרֶם   vineyard (1 Kgs 21:1)

מִשְׁעוֹל   narrow (walled) passage (in vineyard); narrow pathway
(DCH) (Num 22:24 H)

Winepress

יֶקֶב   wine vat; winepress (Walsh); winery, fermentation vat, press
(Jordan) (Prov 3:10)

פּוּרָה   winepress (Walsh); portable winepress (FAJ); winepress, liquid
from winepress (DCH) (Isa 63:3 R)

Dairy

גְּבִינָה   cheese (SDBH) (Job 10:10 H)

חָלָב   milk; fresh milk or processed dairy products (MacDonald);
milk, cheese (DCH) (Gen 49:12)

חֶלְמוּת   egg yolk (SDBH, DCH); possibly mallow plant (Koops)
(Job 6:6 H)

חֶמְאָה   curds (SDBH); curds, butter (DCH) (2 Sam 17:29)

חָרִיץ   cheese (SDBH); full idiom חֲרִצֵי הֶחָלָב = literally "slices of
dairy" (MacDonald) (1 Sam 17:18 R)

שְׁפוֹת   cheese (SDBH) (2 Sam 17:29 H)

Nuts

אֱגוֹז   walnut; nut (Brenner "The Food of Love") (Song 6:11 H)

בָּטְנִים   pistachios; terebinth nuts (Koops) (Gen 43:11 H)

לוּז   hazelnut; almond (Koops) (Gen 30:37 H)

מְשֻׁקָּד   almond (Koops) (Exod 25:33 H)

שָׁקֵד   almond (Gen 43:11 R)

Fruits

אֲבַטִּיחַ   melon; watermelon (Koops) (Num 11:5 H)

אֲבִיּוֹנָה caper plant; caper bush, caper berry (Koops, DCH) (Eccl 12:5 H)

אֶשְׁפָּר date cake (SDBH) (2 Sam 6:19 R)

בְּאָשִׁים fetid fruit (Walsh) (Isa 5:2 H)

בָּכָא unidentified fruit (MacDonald); balsam, or perhaps aspen tree (DCH) (Ps 84:6 R)

בִּכּוּרִים first fruits (of fruits and grain) (Ezek 44:30)

בִּכּוּרָה/בְּכֻּרָה early fig; first fig crop (Borowski *Agriculture*) (Isa 28:4 R)

גַּרְגְּרִים olives (Borowski *Agriculture*); berry, olive, or grape (DCH) (Isa 17:6 H)

דְּבֵלָה pressed fig cake (2 Kgs 20:7 R)

זַיִת olive; olive tree, olive grove (Exod 27:20)

יִצְהָר olive oil; fresh oil (DCH) (Deut 7:13)

מְסֻכָּן mulberry (Koops); mulberry tree or wood, also possibly sisu tree or wood (DCH) (Isa 40:20 H)

נֹקֶף shaking off (olives) (Isa 17:6 R)

עֵץ הָדָר citron (Koops) (Lev 23:40)

פַּג early fig, unripe fig (DCH) (Song 2:13 H)

פְּרֻדֹּת dried figs (Joel 1:17 H)

פְּרִי fruit (Lev 25:19)

קַיִץ late fig, second crop (Borowski *Agriculture*); summer fruits, summer produce (DCH); summer fruit (SDBH) (Jer 8:20)

רִמּוֹן pomegranate (Exod 28:33)

שֶׁמֶן oil tree; wild olive; oleaster (SDBH) (1 Kgs 6:23)

שִׁקְמָה sycamore fig; sycamore tree (DCH) (Isa 9:9 R)

תְּאֵנָה fig; fig tree (DCH) (Gen 3:7)

תֹּמֶר/תְּמֹרָה/תָּמָר date-palm (Exod 15:27 R)

תַּפּוּחַ apple, apricot; peach (Brenner "The Food of Love", Borowski *Agriculture*); quince or apricot (MacDonald); apple tree (DCH) (Prov 25:11 R)

Vegetables

בָּצָל onion (Num 11:5 H)

זֵרוּעַ vegetable (Borowski *Agriculture*); sowing, thing sown (DCH) (Lev 11:37 R)

חָמִיץ chick-pea (?) (Borowski *Agriculture*, Koops); sorrel (DCH) (Isa 30:24 H)

חָצִיר leek; grass; reed (Isa 34:13)

יָרָק vegetable (Borowski *Agriculture*); collective noun meaning herbage, vegetables (DCH) (Deut 11:10 R)

מִקְשָׁה cucumber field; muskmellon, cantalope (Koops) (Isa 1:8 R)

עֲדָשִׁים lentils (2 Sam 17:28 R)

פּוֹל bean; broad bean (MacDonald) (2 Sam 17:28 R)

פְּקָעִים gourds (pl.); gourd-shaped ornament (DCH) (1 Kgs 6:18 R)

קִשָּׁאָה cucumber; muskmellon, cantalope (SDBH, Koops)
(Num 11:5 H)

שׁוּם garlic; used to expel parasites and heal abcesses (Williams)
(Num 11:5 H)

Honey

דְּבַשׁ honey; date honey (Borowski *Agriculture*); bee honey or fruit
honey (MacDonald) (1 Sam 14:25)

יַעַר/יַעֲרָה honeycomb (Brenner "The Food of Love," DCH) (Song 5:1 R)

נֹפֶת honeycomb (Brenner "The Food of Love"); flowing honey
(DCH) (Prov 24:13 R)

צוּף honeycomb (SDBH); mead (Borowski *Daily Life*)
(Ps 19:11 R)

Herbs and Spices, Ointments/Resins/Balms, Incense

Herbs and Spices

אֹרֹת herbs; mallow (DCH) (2 Kgs 4:39 H)

גַּד coriander (Exod 16:31)

דּוּדָאִים mandrake; mandrake, love apple (SDBH) (Gen 30:14–16 R)

חָמִיץ seasoned, salted; chick-pea (?) (Borowski *Agriculture*, Koops);
sorrel (DCH) (Isa 30:24 H)

כַּמֹּן cummin (Isa 28:25 R)

כֻּסֶּמֶת fitches, spelt (Harrison) (Ezek 4:9 R)

מֶלַח salt (Job 6:6)

מֶרְקָחָה spices, seasonings; perfume boiler (כְּלִי); pot of ointment,
spice (DCH) (Job 41:23 R)

מְרֹר bitter herbs (Deut 32:32 R)

נְכֹאת gum tragacanth (Koops) (Gen 37:25 R)

סַם spice; herb (Exod 25:6)

קִנָּמוֹן cinnamon (Exod 30:23 R)

קֶצַח nutmeg (black cummin); fitches, spelt (Harrison); nigella
(Koops); black cumin (DCH) (Isa 28:27 R)

רֶקַח spice (general term) (Song 8:2 H)

Ointments/Resins/Balms

אֲהָלוֹת/אֲהָלִים aloes, agarwood (Num 24:6 R)

בֶּשֶׂם/בְּשֶׂם/בֹּשֶׂם balsam, spices; general term for aromatic spieces, balms
(Nielsen) (Song 5:13)

חֶלְבְּנָה galbanum (resin gum), fennel (Exod 30:34 H)

כֹּפֶר henna (Koops) (Song 1:14 R)

כַּרְכֹּם saffron (Song 4:14 H)

לֹט laudanum (oil), "Rock Rose" (Exod 37:25 R)

מֹר myrrh (Exod 30:23)

נָטָף stacte resin (Exod 30:34 H)

נְכֹאת trangacanth gum; aromatic gum; ladanum (DCH) (Gen 43:11 R)

נֵרְדְּ nard, spikenard (amber-colored oil) (Song 1:12 R)

צֳרִי liquid amber (storax), balm; mastic tree (Harrison); balm, balsam (DCH) (Gen 37:25 R)

קִיקָיוֹן castor-oil tree; gourd (Harrison) (Jonah 4:6 R)

Incense

אֲהָלוֹת/אֲהָלִים aloes, agarwood (Num 24:6 R)

בֹּר hammada plant, used for making soap (Job 9:30 R)

בֶּשֶׂם/בֶּשֶׂם/בֹּשֶׂם balsam, spices; general term for aromatic spieces (Nielsen) (Song 5:13)

לְבוֹנָה/לְבֹנָה frankincense (Jer 6:20)

מֹר myrrh (either dry or wet) (Exod 30:23)

נָטָף stacte resin; used to relieve coughs and stimulate menstruation (Harrison); storax, balm (Nielsen) (Exod 30:34 H)

נְכֹאת gum tragacanth (Koops) (Gen 37:25 R)

סַם spice; herb; general term for aromatic substances (Nielsen) (Exod 25:6)

צֳרִי storax; balm (SDBH) (Gen 37:25 R)

קְטֹרֶת incense; perfume (DCH) (Exod 30:35)

CLOTHING

General Terms

בֶּגֶד	clothing, covering (Gen 24:53)
בִּגְדֵי אַלְמְנוּת	widow's clothing (Gen 38:14) (Pritz)
גְּלוֹם	mantle, clothes, wrapping, wrap; thin garment (Platt) (Ezek 27:24 H)
חֹב	fold (of garment) (SDBH) (Job 31:33 H)
לְבוּשׁ	attire, clothing, garment (Gen 49:11)
מַד	garments; clothing (Pritz) (Lev 6:10 R)
מַחֲלָצוֹת	loin cloth (Platt); outer garment, mantle, cloak (Pritz); festive robe (DCH) (Isa 3:22 R)
מַלְבּוּשׁ	vestments, apparel (Ezek 16:13 R)
מֶלְתָּחָה	royal wardrobe, vestry; clothes store, wardrobe, cloakroom (DCH) (2 Kgs 10:22 H)
מַעֲטֶה	vestment (Isa 61:3 H)
סָדִין	linen wrapper (undergarment) (Judg 14:12–13 R)
סוּת	garment (Gen 49:11 H)
בֶּגֶד עִדִּים	menstrual cloth (SDBH) (Isa 64:5 H)
עוֹר	animal skin (Pritz) (Gen 3:21)
פְּתִיגִיל	some kind of fine garment wrapped around the wearer (Pritz) (Isa 3:24 H)
שֹׁבֶל	garment, clothing (Pritz); skirt (DCH) (Isa 47:2 H)
שִׁית	attire, dress, clothing, garb; mantle (DCH) (Prov 7:10 R)
שַׂלְמָה / שִׂמְלָה	garment, clothing (Pritz) (Exod 22:9)
תִּלְבֹּשֶׁת	a garment (Isa 59:17 H)

Old Clothes

בְּלוֹי	rag (SDBH) (Jer 38:11 R)
מֶלַח	old clothes, rags (SDBH) (Jer 38:11)
קְרָעִים	torn pieces of cloth, rags, tattered clothes (SDBH) (Prov 23:21 R)

Outer Garment

כְּסוּת	covering, garment (Pritz) (Exod 21:10 R)
מִכְנָסַיִם	breeches, drawers (SDBH) (Exod 28:42 R)
מִכְסֶה	covering, garment (Exod 26:14)
שַׂלְמָה/שִׂמְלָה/ סַלְמָה	outer garment; cloak, mantle (DCH) (Deut 29:4)

Robe

מַכְלֻל ornate robe; perfect (Ezek 27:24 H)

מַעֲטָפָת enveloping cape (Platt); cape, mantle, cloak (SDBH) (Isa 3:22 H)

מְעִיל robe (SDBH) (Exod 28:4)

תַּכְרִיךְ long royal robe, mantle (Esther); cloth wrapping, garment (Hurvitz) (Esth 8:15 H)

Band

אֲפֵר band, bandage, cloth (SDBH) (1 Kgs 20:38 R)

אַבְנֵט sash (SDBH) (Exod 28:4 R)

אֵזוֹר belt, band; loincloth, waistcloth (SDBH) (Job 12:18 H)

חֲגוֹר girdle, belt (SDBH) (Gen 3:7 R)

חֲגוֹרָה loincloth (Pritz); belt (DCH) (Gen 3:7 R)

חֵשֶׁב girdle, band (Exod 28:8 R)

חֲתֻלָּה swaddling band (SDBH) (Job 38:9 H)

כֶּסֶת band for wrist or arm (SDBH); wristband, magic charm (Pritz) (Ezek 13:18 R)

מֵזַח waistband, sash, belt (Pritz); girdle (DCH) (Ps 109:19 H)

סָדִין warriors' belts (Platt); linen garment (DCH) (Isa 3:23 R)

קִשֻּׁרִים sashes, bridal bands; sashes, girdles, ribbons (SDBH) (Isa 3:20 R)

Tunic

כֻּתֹּנֶת tunic, shirt, undergarment (Gen 3:21)

מַעֲטָפָת overtunic, mantle, cloak (Isa 3:22 H)

סָדִין shirt, tunic (Pritz) (Prov 31:24 R)

פַּס long-sleeved tunic; variously colored material (DCH) (Gen 37:3 R)

Hem/Fringes

גְּדִלִים fringes, tassels of garment (Pritz) (Deut 22:12 R)

כָּנָף hem, corner of garment (Pritz) (Num 15:38)

צִיצָת fringes, tassels of garment (Pritz) (Num 15:38 R)

שׁוּל hem, skirt (of robe), bottom edge; train of garment (Pritz) (Exod 28:33)

Cloak

אַדֶּרֶת cloak, mantle, robe (SDBH) (Gen 25:25)

מִטְפַּחַת cloak, spreading garment, wide cloak (Ruth 3:15 R)

תַּכְרִיךְ mantle, cape, cloak (Pritz) (Esth 8:15 H)

Head Covering

טְבוּל	turban (Ezek 23:15 H)
טוֹטָפוֹת	frontlet, phylactery, headband, sign, mark, reminder (SDBH) (Exod 13:16 R)
כֶּתֶר	circlet, diadem, crown (Persian) (Esth 1:11 R)
לִוְיָה	wreath, garland (SDBH) (Prov 1:9 R)
מִגְבָּעָה	mitre (priest), headband (Exod 28:40 R)
מִצְנֶפֶת	turban, diadem, tiara (Ezek 21:26)
נֵזֶר	crown, headband (king, high priest) (Exod 29:6)
עֲטָרָה	crown, royal diadem (2 Sam 12:30)
פְּאֵר	headwrap, turban (Isa 3:20 R)
צִיץ	(golden) plate, disk, frontlet, medallion on high priest's turban (SDBH) (Exod 28:36)
צָנִיף	headdress (men, priest, women) (Isa 3:23 R)
צְפִירָה	crown, wreath (Isa 28:5 H)

Veils

מַסְוֶה	face covering (Exod 34:33–35 R)
מִסְפָּחָה / מִטְפַּחַת	long veil, scarf (Ezek 13:18 R)
צַמָּה	woman's veil (Song 4:1 R)
צָעִיף	shawl, wrapper, veil (Gen 24:65 R)
רְדִיד	cloak, large veil (Isa 3:23 R)
רְעָלוֹת	veils ("tremulous"); beads (Platt) (Isa 3:19 H)

Footwear

מִצְחָת	greaves (1 Sam 17:6 H)
נַעַל	sandal (Gen 14:23)
סְאוֹן	military boot (Isa 9:4 H)
שְׂרוֹךְ	thong (sandal); strap of sandal (Pritz) (Gen 14:23 R)

Jewelry

General

חֲלִי / חֶלְיָה	ornament, jewel (SDBH) (Prov 25:12 R)
לְחָשִׁים	snake charms (Platt); amulets (DCH) (Isa 3:20 R)
עֲדִי	jewelry, ornaments (2 Sam 1:24)
רְעָלוֹת	veils ('tremulous'); beads (Platt) (Isa 3:19 H)
תִּפְאֶרֶת	jewelry, beauty; insignia of office (Platt) (Isa 3:18 R)

Head

פְּאֵר	garland crown (Platt); headdress, turban (DCH) (Isa 3:20 R)
שְׁבִיסִים	sun- or star-disks (Platt); women's jewelry in the shape of the sun (DCH) (Isa 3:18 H)

שַׁהֲרֹן crescent (Platt); crescent, little moon (DCH) (Isa 3:18 R)

תּוֹר ornament (SDBH); plait, earring, pendant (DCH) (Song 1:10 R)

Ear

נְטִיפָה pendant (ear) (Isa 3:19 R)

עָגִיל earring (Num 31:50 R)

Nose

חָח nose ring, hook; fibula, brooch (DCH) (Exod 35:22 R)

נֶזֶם nose ring (Prov 11:22)

Neck

בַּיִת house; sachet of perfume worn around neck by women (כְּלִי); container (of perfume) (DCH) (Isa 3:20)

חָח brooch, pin (SDBH) (Exod 35:22)

חֲרוּזִים string of jewels, string of shells (SDBH) (Song 1:10 H)

כּוּמָז neck ornament (golden) (Num 31:50 R)

עֲנָק necklace, collar (Prov 1:9 R)

צַוְּרֹן necklace (SDBH) (Song 4:9 H)

רְבִיד necklace, neck-chain (Gen 41:42 R)

שַׂהֲרֹן crescent, neck pendant (Judg 8:26 R)

Arm

צָמִיד arm-clasp, bracelet (Gen 24:22 R)

צְעָדוֹת armlets (Platt); armband (DCH) (Isa 3:20 H)

Wrist

שֵׁירוֹת wrist-bands; necklace cords (Platt); bracelets, bangles (DCH) (Isa 3:19 H)

Ring/Seal

גָּלִיל rod, ring (DCH) (Esth 1:6 R)

חוֹתָם signature-ring, seal (Gen 38:18)

חֹתֶמֶת signet-ring, seal (Gen 38:25 H)

טַבַּעַת seal, signet, ring (Isa 3:21)

Ankle

אֶצְעָדָה ankle chain, step chain; bracelet (Num 31:50 R)

עֶכֶס anklet, bangle (Isa 3:18 R)

צְעָדָה ankle chain (Isa 3:20 R)

Fabric

אֵטוּן thread, yarn; linen (Prov 7:16 H)

בַּד linen (Exod 28:42)

בּוּץ cotton, byssus; fine undyed linen (CT) (1 Chr 4:21 R)

בְּרֹמִים two-colored fabric, variegated cloth (Ezek 27:24 H)

דְּמֶשֶׁק damask (Amos 3:12 H)

חוּר white linen (Esth 1:6 R)

חֲטֻבוֹת multi-colored embroidered cloth, dark-hued stuff; also considered beautiful (SDBH) (Prov 7:16 H)

חֹפֶשׁ material; saddle-clothes; woven material (DCH) (Ezek 27:20 H)

כַּרְפַּס white linen, cotton cloth (Esth 1:6 H)

מַטְוֶה yarn (SDBH) (Exod 35:25 H)

מַכְבֵּר netted cloth (thick) (2 Kgs 8:15 H)

מֶשִׁי fine fabric (Ezek 16:10 R)

עוֹר leather, skin; hide of animals, skin of humans (DCH) (Gen 27:16)

עֵרֶב woof, web; woven or knitted material (SDBH) (Lev 13:58 R)

פְּלָדָה cloth (SDBH); covering, blanket, caparison (Nah 2:4 H)

פִּשְׁתָּה linen, flax (Exod 9:31 R)

צֶבַע dyed cloth (SDBH) (Judg 5:30 R)

צֶמֶר wool (Lev 13:47)

קְרָעִים torn pieces of cloth, rags, tattered clothes (SDBH) (1 Kgs 11:30 R)

רִקְמָה/רֶקֶם colorful weaving; embroidered cloth, needlework (SDBH) (Judg 5:30)

שַׁעַטְנֵז mixed linen and wool (Lev 19:19 R)

שֵׁשׁ fine undyed linen (CT); byssus, linen (DCH) (Gen 41:42)

שְׁתִי warp (weaving); woven or knitted material (SDBH) (Lev 13:48 R)

Cosmetics

Eyes

כחל paint eyes with stibium (Ezek 23:40 H)

פּוּךְ black eyeshadow (stibium), dye; antimony, malachite, eye makeup (DCH) (2 Kgs 9:30 R)

מְשַׂקְּרוֹת applying makeup to eyes (CT) (Isa 3:16 H)

Application

מְרוּקִים cosmetics, scraping, rubbing; cosmetic treatment (DCH) (Esth 2:12 H)

Ointment/Perfume

אֲבָקָה fragrant powders (SDBH) (Song 3:6 H)

בֶּשֶׂם/בְּשָׂם/בֹּשֶׂם spices, perfume, balsam oil (SDBH) (Exod 25:6)

בָּתֵּי הַנֶּפֶשׁ tubular "soul" cases (Platt) (Isa 3:20)

כֹּפֶר henna (CT) (Song 1:14 R)

כַּרְכֹּם saffron fragrance (CT) (Song 4:14 H)

לֹט ladanum (used in perfume) (SDBH) (Gen 37:25 R)

מְקֻטָּר perfume, incense (SDBH) (Mal 1:11 H)

מִרְקַחַת ointment, perfumery (Exod 30:25)

נֵרְדְּ nard, spikenard (SDBH) (Song 1:12 R)

נֶשֶׁק pleasant scents (SDBH) (1 Kgs 10:25 R)

צֳרִי storax, balm (SDBH) (Gen 37:25 R)

קְטֹרֶת perfume, incense (SDBH) (Exod 25:6)

קִנָּמוֹן cinnamon (SDBH) (Exod 30:23 R)

קְצִיעוֹת / קְצִיעָה cassia (SDBH) (Ps 45:9 H)

רַקָּח ointment maker, perfume (Neh 3:8 H)

רַקָּחָה / רַקָּח perfumer (1 Sam 8:13 H)

שֶׁמֶן oil, fat (Deut 33:24)

Mirror

גִּלָּיוֹן mirror; tablet; papyrus garment (DCH) (Isa 3:23 H)

רְאִי mirror (Job 37:18 H)

מַרְאָה mirror; vision (Exod 38:8)

PART III

THE SOCIAL ORDER

FAMILY AND KINSHIP

Immediate Family

Father/Husband

אָב   father (Gen 2:24)

אִישׁ   man, husband (Gen 2:24)

בַּעַל   husband (Deut 24:4)

Wife/Mother

אֵם   mother (Gen 2:24)

אֵשֶׁת/אִשָּׁה   wife, woman (Gen 16:3)

Son

בֵּן   son (Gen 3:16)

בַּר   son (SDBH) (Prov 31:2)

יָלִיד   son, born (Gen 17:12)

Daughter

בְּכִירָה   eldest daughter (Gen 19:33 R)

בַּת   daughter (Gen 20:12)

Brother/Sister

אָח   brother (Gen 4:2); nephew (Gen 14:14) (Rattray)

אָחוֹת   sister; sister, half-sister (SDBH) (Gen 4:22)

בֶּן־אָח   son of brother, nephew (Rattray) (Gen 12:5)

Uncle/Aunt

בֶּן־דֹּד   son of uncle, male cousin (Lev 25:49)

דּוֹד   uncle, father's brother (Lev 10:4)

דּוֹדָה   aunt, father's brother's wife; father's sister (Rattray) (Exod 6:20 R)

Firstborn

בְּכוֹר   firstborn (SDBH) (Gen 4:4)

בְּכִירָה   eldest daughter (Gen 19:33 R)

בְּכֹרָה   right of firstborn (SDBH) (Gen 25:31)

Relatives/Kin/Offspring

מֹדָע/מֹדַעַת   relative, kinsman, kinswoman (DCH) (Ruth 2:1 R)

נֶכֶד (with נִין)   offspring; descendents, posterity (SDBH); progeny (DCH) (Gen 21:23)

עֵקֶר   family member; offshoot (SDBH) (Lev 25:47 H)

שְׁאֵר בָּשָׂר   "near in flesh," close kin (Rattray) (Lev 18:6)

תּוֹאֲמִים/תְאוֹמִים   twins (DCH) (Gen 25:24 R)

In-Laws

חָם father-in-law; father-in-law (of women) (Rattray) (Gen 38:13 R)

חָמוֹת mother-in-law; mother-in-law (of woman) (Rattray) (Ruth 1:14)

חֹתֵן father-in-law (SDBH); father-in-law (of men) (Rattray) (Exod 3:1)

חָתָן groom, son-in-law, daughter's husband; bridegroom (DCH) (Exod 4:25)

חֹתֶנֶת mother-in-law (SDBH); mother-in-law (of men) (Rattray) (Deut 27:23 H)

יָבָם brother-in-law; husband's brother (DCH) (Deut 25:5 R)

יְבָמָה sister-in-law (Ruth 1:15 R)

כַּלָּה bride, daughter-in-law, son's wife (Gen 11:31)

Marriage/Divorce

גֹּאֵל kinsman, redeemer (Ruth 3:13)

חתן to give away in marriage (Gen 34:9)

כְּלוּלֹת betrothal (as bride) (Jer 2:2 H)

מֹהַר bride-price (Gen 34:12 R)

פִּילֶגֶשׁ concubine (SDBH) (Gen 22:24)

צָרָה rival-wife (SDBH) (1 Sam 1:6 H)

שִׁלּוּחִים divorce, bill of divorce (Exod 18:2 R)

שָׂרָה princess, noble woman; mistress (SDBH) (Judg 5:29 R)

Widowhood

אַלְמָנָה widow (Lev 22:13)

אַלְמָנוּת widowhood (2 Sam 20:3 R)

יבם to marry a brother's widow (Gen 38:8 R)

Family/Clan

בֵּית־אָב family, "house of the father" (2 Chr 35:5)

יַחַשׂ genealogy, family list, pedigree (Neh 7:5 H)

מוֹלֶדֶת lineage, offspring, family, relations (Ezek 16:3)

מִשְׁפָּחָה family, clan (Gen 8:19)

תּוֹלְדוֹת descent, family, history (Gen 5:1)

WORSHIP/CULTIC

Structures

אֹהֶל הָעֵדוּת   tent of witness (Num 9:15)

אֹהֶל־מוֹעֵד   Tent of Meeting (Exod 27:21)

דְּבִיר   innermost sanctuary, shrine (1 Kgs 6:19)

הֵיכָל   temple (Hos 8:14)

מִשְׁכָּן   tabernacle, sanctuary; dwelling-place (2 Sam 7:6)

Ark of the Covenant

אֲרוֹן   ark of covenant, chest, box (Exod 30:6)

בַּד   pole (for side of ark) (Pritz); carrying-pole (כלי) (Exod 25:13)

בֵּית הַכַּפֹּרֶת   Holy of Holies (Hurvitz) (1 Chr 28:11)

זֵר   rim, molding (of ark) (Pritz) (Exod 25:11)

טַבְּעֹת   rings (of gold, for ark) (Pritz) (Exod 25:12)

בֵּית־קֹדֶשׁ הַקֳּדָשִׁים   Holy of Holies (Hurvitz) (2 Chr 3:8)

כַּף   incense dish (Pritz); handbowl, incense-ladle (כלי) (Exod 25:29)

כַּפֹּרֶת   Mercy seat, cover/lid of ark (Pritz) (Exod 25:17)

כְּרוּב / כְּרֻבִים   cherubim on lid of ark (Pritz) (Exod 25:18)

מוֹט   pole, frame; pole (for side of ark) (Pritz); yoke (כלי) (Num 4:10 R)

מְנַקִּית   jars (for wine offerings) (Pritz) (Exod 25:29 R)

פַּעַם   leg of table (Pritz) (Exod 25:12)

צֶלַע   side (of ark) (Pritz) (Exod 25:12)

קַשְׂוָה   jug, jar (libations); jug, jar, flagon, pitcher (SDBH) (Exod 25:29 R)

Altars

אֲרִיאֵל / הַרְאֵל   altar, hearth (Ezek 43:15 R)

בַּד   pole (for side of Tabernacle altar) (Pritz) (Exod 27:6–7)

טַבַּעַת   ring (of Tabernacle altar) (Pritz) (Exod 27:4)

כַּרְכֹּב   rim, ledge of altar (Pritz) (Exod 27:5 R)

לְבֵנִים   incense altars (Pritz) (Isa 65:3)

מוֹקְדָה   altar top, altar-plate (for burnt offering) (Lev 6:2 H)

מִזְבֵּחַ   sacrificial altar (Gen 8:20)

מִכְבָּר   grating of Tabernacle altar (Pritz) (Exod 27:4 R)

מִקְטָר   hearth, incense stand (Exod 30:1 H)

קַרְנֹת   horns of the altar (Pritz) (Exod 27:2)

שֻׁלְחָן   altar, table, incense altar, table for consecrated bread, table for preparing sacrificial victims (Pritz) (Mal 1:7)

Menorah/Lampstand

גָּבִיעַ   cup at the top of each stem, for holding candles (Pritz) (Exod 25:31)

יָרֵךְ   base of lampstand (Pritz) (Exod 25:31)

מְנֹרָה / מְנוֹרָה   menorah, lampstand (Pritz) (Exod 25:31 – 35)

פֶּרַח   flower-shaped decoration on each cup (Pritz) (Exod 25:31)

קָנֶה   arm, stem of lampstand (Pritz) (Exod 25:31)

Personnel

הֹזֶה   seer; dreamer (DCH) (Isa 56:10 H)

כֹּהֵן   priest (Lev 6:15)

כְּהֻנָּה   priesthood (Exod 29:9)

מַכָּר   business accessor, temple official valuing sacrifices (DCH) (2 Kgs 12:6 R)

מָשְׁחָה   anointing, being anointed (Exod 40:15 R)

מִשְׁמֶרֶת   ceremonial office, duty, service (Gen 26:5)

נְבִיאָה/נָבִיא   prophet (Deut 18:15)

נָזִיר   devoted one; Nazirite (Gen 49:26)

נְתוּנִים   those assigned (Ezra 8:17)

עָתָר   worshipper, suppliant; odor, incense (Zeph 3:10 H)

פְּקֻדָּה   office, appointment, commission (Num 3:36)

רֹאֶה   seer; vision (1 Sam 9:9)

Garb (Priestly)

אַבְנֵט   sash, girdle (undergarment) (Exod 28:4 R)

אֵפֹד/אֵפוֹד   ephod, shoulder-piece, high-priest's shoulder-cape (Exod 25:7)

חֵשֶׁב   band (on ephod); girdle of ephod (DCH) (Exod 28:8 R)

חֹשֶׁן   breastplate, pocket (Exod 25:7)

כְּתֹנֶת   tunic, shirt (Pritz) (Exod 28:4)

מִגְבָּעָה   headband, mitre (Exod 28:40 R)

מַד   priestly robe (Ps 133:2 R)

מִכְנָסִים   leggings, breeches (Exod 28:42 R)

מְעִיל   priestly robe (Pritz) (Exod 28:4)

מִצְנֶפֶת   mitre, turban (Exod 28:4)

פְּאֵר   turban, headdress (Pritz) (Exod 39:28 R)

פַּעֲמֹן / פַּעֲמוֹן   bells (sewn in hem of priestly robe) (Exod 28:33 – 34 R)

צִיץ   forehead plate (Pritz) (Exod 28:36)

צָנִיף   turban, headdress (Pritz) (Zech 3:5 R)

Accoutrements

(For Bowls, etc., see Containers and Implements)

בֶּגֶד	tablecloth, covering (Num 4:6)
יָם	water tank in Temple (Pritz) (1 Kgs 7:23–25)
יָע	shovel; fire-shovel (DCH) (Exod 27:3 R)
כִּיֹר / כִּיר	washstand, basin, bowl (Pritz) (1 Kgs 7:30)
מַזְלֵג	fork (three-pronged) (Pritz) (1 Sam 2:13–14 R)
מְזַמְּרֹות	snuffers, wick trimmers (Pritz) (1 Kgs 7:50 R)
מַחְתָּה	fire-pan, censer; small shovel, firepan (Pritz) (Exod 25:38)
מְכֹונָה	moveable stand (Pritz); base, stand (DCH) (1 Kgs 7:27)
מֶלְקָחַיִם	snuffers, tongs; forceps, tongs (כלי) (Exod 25:38 R)
מַעֲצָד	tongs (Pritz) (Isa 44:12 R)
מִקְטֶרֶת	censer, coal-pan (2 Chr 26:19 R)
קְעָרָה	plate (as implement in Tabernacle) (Pritz) (Exod 25:29)

Vow

אִסָּר	vow of abstinence, binding obligation (Num 30:5)
נֶדֶר	vow (Num 30:5)

Sacrifices and Offerings

אַזְכָּרָה	memorial offering; token offering (DCH) (Lev 5:12 R)
אִשֶּׁה	burnt offering, sacrifice (Exod 29:25)
אָשָׁם	guilt-offering (1 Sam 6:4)
הַבְהָב	gift, offering (Hos 8:13 H)
זֶבַח	sacrifice (Exod 34:15)
חַטָּאָה	sacrifice, offense; sin (DCH) (Gen 20:9 R)
חֲטָאָה	sin-offering; offense (Exod 34:7 R)
מִנְחָה	donation, tribute, offering (Gen 32:21)
מִשְׁחָה	consecrated portion (Num 18:8 H)
מַתָּנָה	present, sacrificial offering (Num 18:7)
נְדָבָה	voluntary offering (Exod 35:29)
נִיחֹוחַ	aroma (of sacrifice) (Ezek 6:13)
נֶסֶךְ	libation, drink offering (Num 28:14)
עֹלָה	whole burnt offering (Exod 29:42)
קָרְבָּן	offering, sacrificial present, gift (Lev 1:2)
רֵיחַ	aroma, odor, fragrance (Gen 8:21)
שֶׁלֶם	peace offering (Num 7:17)
שָׁרֵת	ritual service (Num 4:12 R)
תֹּודָה	sacrifice of thanksgiving; adoration, praise (Josh 7:19)
תְּנוּפָה	wave-offering, brandishing (Num 8:11)

תְּרוּמָה present, sacrifice, tribute, heave offering (Num 15:19)

תְּרוּמִיָּה sacrificial offering, contribution (Ezek 48:12 H)

Idolatry

אֶבֶן מַשְׂכִּית carved stone, idol (Pritz) (Lev 26:1)

אֱלִיל worthless, vain, idol (Lev 19:4)

אֲשֵׁרָה Asherah, goddess images (Pritz) (Exod 34:13)

בָּמָה high place (shrine, altar) (Lev 26:30)

בַּעַל Baal, lord, husband (Judg 6:31)

גִּלּוּל idol (Lev 26:30)

זְנוּת/זְנוּנִים/תַּזְנוּת idolatry, harlotry (Num 14:33 R)

חַמָּן sun-pillar, altar; incense altar (DCH) (Lev 26:30 R)

כַּוָּנִים sacred cakes for false gods (Pritz) (Jer 7:18 R)

כִּיּוּן statue for deity (Saturn/Kivvun) (Amos 5:26 H)

כֹּמֶר idolatrous priest; priests of foreign cults (DCH) (Hos 10:5 R)

מְלֶכֶת Queen (of Heaven) (Jer 7:18 R)

מַסֵּכָה molten image (Judg 17:4)

מַצֵּבָה stone pillar (Lev 26:1)

מַשְׂכִּית carved image (Lev 26:1)

נֶסֶךְ cast idol; libation; molten image (Pritz) (Isa 41:29)

סֶמֶל idol, image (Pritz) (Ezek 8:3 R)

פָּסִיל graven image (Deut 7:5)

פֶּסֶל idol; graven image (Pritz) (Lev 26:1)

צִירִים idols (Pritz) (Isa 45:16 R)

צֶלֶם idol, image (Num 33:52)

שִׁקּוּץ idol, detestable thing (Deut 29:16)

תַּבְנִית idol, image (Pritz) (Ps 106:20)

תְּרָפִים Teraphim, household idols (Pritz) (Gen 31:19)

Divination

אוֹב medium, necromancer; ghost (DCH) (1 Sam 28:3)

אִטִּים ghosts (Isa 19:3 H)

אוּרִים lots, dice, stones ("lights"); Urim (DCH) (Exod 28:30 R)

אַשָּׁף enchanter, conjurer; exorcist (DCH) (Dan 1:20 R)

גּוֹרָל lot, stone (Josh 15:1)

חֶבֶר spell, enchantment; noise, spell, incantation (DCH) (Deut 18:11 R)

חֹבֵר spellcaster (Ps 58:6 R)

חֲכַם חֲרָשִׁים sorcerer, lit. "wise one of sorceries" (DCH) (Isa 3:3 H)

חַרְטֹם magician, astrologer (Exod 9:11)

יִדְּעֹנִי soothsayer, spirit; familiar spirit, medium, necromancer (DCH) (1 Sam 28:3)

כַּשָּׁף sorcerer (Jer 27:9 H)

מְכַשֵּׁף sorcerer, magician (Deut 18:10 R)

מְנַחֵשׁ omen interpreter; diviner (DCH) (Deut 18:10)

מְעוֹנֵן enchanter; diviner of thunder (Mic 5:12 R)

מִקְסָם augury, divination (Ezek 12:24 R)

נַחַשׁ omen; divination (Num 24:1 R)

קֶסֶם prediction, divination, oracle (Ezek 21:27)

רְפָאִים deceased, ghost, shade, spirit (Isa 26:14 R)

תֻּמִּים lots, dice, stones ("perfections"); Thummin (DCH)
(Exod 28:30 R)

Dream/Vision/Oracle

חָזוֹן sight, vision, oracle (1 Sam 3:1)

חָזוּת oracle, vision (Isa 21:2 R)

חִזָּיוֹן dream, revelation, vision (Job 20:8 R)

חֲלוֹם dream, vision (Isa 29:7)

מַחֲזֶה vision (Num 24:4 R)

מַרְאָה/מַרְאֶה vision, revelation (Ezek 43:3)

מַשָּׂא oracle; burden, load (Isa 13:1)

נְבוּאָה prophecy, prophetic utterance/writing (Hurvitz) (Neh 6:12 R)

נְאֻם utterance, oracle (Amos 2:11)

פִּתְרוֹן interpretation (Gen 40:12 R)

Purity/Impurity

Pure

טָהוֹר pure (Num 19:9)

טָהֳרָה ritual purity, purification, cleansing (1 Chr 23:28)

כִּפֻּרִים atonement (Lev 23:27 R)

נָקִי innocent, clean (Deut 24:5)

קָדוֹשׁ holy, sacred (1 Sam 6:20)

קֹדֶשׁ sacredness, holiness (Joel 4:17)

Impure

זָר profane, strange, foreign (Lev 22:12)

חֹל profane; profaneness (DCH) (Ezek 48:15 R)

חָלִילָה God forbid! Far be it! (Gen 18:25)

חֲנֻפָּה impiety, pollution (Jer 23:15 H)

טָמֵא impure (Num 18:15)

טֻמְאָה religious impurity (Lev 15:25)

נִדָּה menstrual impurity, uncleanness (Ezek 36:17)

פִּגּוּל foul, ritually impure; meat unfit for use (DCH) (Lev 7:18 R)

Circumcision

מוּל to circumcise (Deut 30:6)

מוּלָה circumcision (DCH) (Exod 4:26 H)

מְכֵרָה circumcision blade (DCH) (Gen 49:5 H)

מָלַל to circumcise, cut off (DCH) (Josh 5:2 R)

נָמוּל circumcised (Exod 4:26)

עָרֵל uncircumcised (Judg 14:3)

עָרְלָה foreskin (Deut 10:16)

Assembly

מַקְהֵל assembly, choir (Ps 26:12 R)

מִקְרָא assembly, convocation (Lev 23:21)

עֵדָה congregation, gathering (Num 16:5)

עֲצָרָה solemn assembly (Lev 23:36)

קָהָל assembly, congregation (Num 22:4)

קְהִלָּה assembly, congregation (Deut 33:4 R)

Holidays/Festivals

חַג feast, festival (SDBH) (Exod 10:9)

חַג הָאָסִף Feast of the Harvest (Borowski *Agriculture*) (Exod 23:16)

חַג הַמַּצּוֹת Feast of Unleavened Bread, Passover (Borowski *Agriculture*) (Exod 23:15)

חַג סֻכּוֹת Festival of Sukkoth; Feast of Booths (Borowski *Agriculture*) (Lev 23:34)

חַג שָׁבֻעֹת Feast of Weeks (Borowski *Agriculture*) (Exod 34:22)

חֹדֶשׁ New Moon (1 Sam 20:5)

יוֹם הַכִּפֻּרִים Day of Atonement (Lev 23:27–28)

עֲצָרָה festival, holiday (Joel 1:14)

פּוּרִים lots, small pebbles used to decide questions, Purim (SDBH) (Esth 9:28 R)

פֶּסַח Passover (Exod 12:11)

שַׁבָּת Sabbath (Exod 16:23)

LAW AND COVENANT
Laws/Decrees

בְּרִית covenant, treaty, agreement (Gen 17:7)

דָּבָר word, matter, speech; dispute, controversy case, case decided in court, legal decision (Bovati) (Exod 22:8)

דָּת royal edict, decree (Esth 2:8)

חֹק rule, statute (Exod 18:16)

חֻקָּה statute, ordinance (Deut 6:2)

חֵרֶם ban, devoted to destruction (Deut 13:17)

מַאֲמַר word, commandment, decree (Esth 1:15 R)

מִצְוָה commandment, law (Isa 29:13)

מִשְׁפָּט legal decision, sentence, law (Deut 16:18)

פִּקּוּדִים precepts, commandments (Ps 19:9)

פְּרִיץ duty, law (DCH) (Ps 17:4 H)

פִּתְגָם edict, sentence; decree, word (Hurvitz) (Eccl 8:11 R)

צַו precept (Hos 5:11 R)

עֵדֹת treaty stipulations (Van der Toorn) (Deut 4:45 R)

קַו law, precept, statute (DCH) (Ps 19:5)

שָׁפָט law, penalty; verdict of court (Bovati) (Exod 12:12)

תּוֹרָה instruction, precept, Torah (Isa 1:10)

Oath/Blessing/Curse

אָלָה oath; curse; covenant or treaty, curses from breaking covenant or treaty (Aitken) (Deut 29:19 R)

אלה to swear an oath, to curse (Aitken) (1 Kgs 8:31)

ארר to curse (Aitken) (Gen 4:11 R)

ברך to bless, (euphemistically) to curse (Aitken) (1 Sam 25:33)

בְּרָכָה blessing, praise, something beneficial (Aitken) (Prov 24:25)

זעם to utter a curse, denounce (Aitken) (Isa 66:14)

נקב to curse, to utter (Aitken "נָקַב II") (Lev 24:11 R)

קבב to curse (Aitken) (Num 22:11)

קלל to curse, call down evil on someone (Aitken) (1 Sam 17:43)

קְלָלָה curse (Gen 27:12)

שְׁבוּעָה oath (Neh 10:30)

תַּאֲלָה curse (Lam 3:65 H)

Justice

אִישׁ רִיב defendant, accused (Bovati) (Judg 12:2)

אִישׁ רִיבִי plaintiff, accuser (Bovati) (Job 31:35)

גֹּאֵל הַדָּם avenger of blood (Bovati) (Num 35:19)

דַּיָּן   judge (Bovati) (1 Sam 24:15 R)

דִּין   judgment, cause, lawsuit; lawsuits concerning property or other civil matters (Bovati) (Jer 5:28)

שפט   to enter into a controversy with someone, be at odds legally (Bovati) (Deut 16:18)

יָפֵחַ   witness (Bovati) (Prov 12:17 R)

יָרִיב   plaintiff, accuser (Bovati) (Isa 49:25 H)

כֹּפֶר   monetary compensation in legal case (Bovati); ransom (DCH) (Exod 21:30)

מַזְכִּיר   misdeed (legal) (Bovati); recorder (DCH) (Gen 41:9)

מִישׁוֹר   equity, justice (Isa 11:4)

מְרִיב   plaintiff, accuser (Bovati); contention (DCH) (1 Sam 2:10 R)

נטה   to pervert justice (Bovati) (Deut 16:19)

עֵד   witness in court, usually for prosecution (Bovati) (Lev 5:1)

פָּלִיל   magistrate, judge (Bovati) (Deut 32:31 R)

פְּלִילָה   justice, right; judgment, responsibility, decision, intervention (DCH) (Isa 16:3 H)

צַדִּיק   just one; innocent (Bovati) (Jer 12:1)

צְדָקָה   justice, righteousness (Ps 112:3)

רִיב   legal controversy that takes place between two persons (Bovati); argument, case, strife, dispute (DCH); to strive, contend, bring a lawsuit (Gen 13:7)

שֹׁפֵט/שֹׁפְטָה   judge (Bovati) (Judg 4:4)

Crime/Evil/Wrong

חֵטְא   crime, penalty (Hos 12:9)

חַטָּא   criminal, wrongdoer (Ps 51:15)

חֲטָאָה   wrong, offense (Gen 20:9 R)

חָמָס   violence, wrong (Jer 6:7)

סָרָה   crime, apostasy, offense (Deut 13:6 R)

עַוָּתָה   oppression, wrong (Lam 3:59 H)

רַע   bad, evil (Prov 9:16)

רָשָׁע   evildoer; rich (DCH) (Prov 11:7 H)

רִשְׁעָה/רֶשַׁע   wrong, wickedness, injustice (Mic 6:11)

שְׁגָגָה   error, inadvertent sin (Lev 5:15)

שֶׁקֶר   lie, falsehood (Exod 5:9)

Freedom

גאל   to redeem oneself, free oneself (SDBH) (Lev 25:49)

גְּאֻלָּה   redemption (SDBH) (Lev 25:24)

דְּרוֹר   freedom (Lev 25:10 R)

חֻפְשָׁה   freedom, liberty (Lev 19:20 H)

Poor/Oppressed

אֶבְיוֹן	beggar, poor, needy (Exod 23:6)
דַּל / דַּלָּה	poor, thin (Exod 23:3)
חָלוּף	helpless people, destitute people (SDBH); passing away, opposition, foolishness (DCH) (Prov 31:8 H)
מוּךְ	to be, become poor (SDBH); to be low (DCH) (Lev 25:25 R)
מַחְסוֹר	impoverishment; lack (DCH) (Prov 6:11)
מִסְכֵּן	poor, indigent (Eccl 4:13 H)
מִסְכֵּנֻת	poverty (Deut 8:9 H)
עָנָו / עָנִי	oppressed, poor, humiliated (Prov 22:22)
עַרְעָר	naked, poor, helpless; destitute (DCH) (Ps 102:18 H)
פְּרָזוֹן	peasantry (SDBH) (Judg 5:7 R)
רָאשִׁים / רָשׁ / רוּשׁ	poor, destitute, needy (1 Sam 8:23)

Wealthy/Rich

חַשְׁמַן	nobles (SDBH); envoy, bronze, red cloth (DCH) (Ps 68:32 H)
נָדִיב	noble person (SDBH) (Num 21:18)
עֹשֶׁר	wealth, riches (Esth 1:4)
פַּרְתְּמִים	nobles (SDBH) (Esth 1:3 R)
שׁוֹעַ	rich, noble (SDBH) (Job 34:19 R)

PROFESSIONS AND OCCUPATIONS

(For Religious Professions, see Worship/Cultic ➡ Personnel)

Government: Leaders

(See also Military)

Royal Family

גְּבִירָה   queen, queen-mother; woman who is in a position of authority over another person as a legal owner, employer, or sovereign (SDBH) (Gen 16:4)

מֶלֶךְ   king (Gen 14:1)

מַלְכָּה   queen (1 Kgs 10:1)

שֵׁגַל   queen (SDBH) (Ps 45:10 R)

שַׁלִּיט   prince, warrior; ruler, governor (DCH) (Eccl 7:19 R)

שָׂרָה   princess, female noble (Esth 1:18 R)

Nobility

חֹר   noble, nobility (SDBH) (1 Kgs 21:8)

נָדִיב   noble person (SDBH) (Num 21:18)

General

אַבִּיר   chief (SDBH); mighty one, hero (DCH) (1 Sam 21:8)

אָדוֹן   lord; master; owner (SDBH) (Gen 18:12)

אַלּוּף   chieftain (Gen 36:15)

גְּבִיר   lord; master (SDBH) (Gen 27:29 R)

מִמְשָׁל   ruler; dominion, rule (DCH) (Dan 11:3 R)

מִנְזָר   courtier, prince (Nah 3:17 H)

נָגִיד   leader, commander, prince (2 Chr 6:5)

נְצִיב   governor (SDBH) (1 Kgs 4:19)

נָשִׂיא   ruler, king, leader; prince (DCH) (Gen 34:2)

סֶגֶן   prefect; ruler (DCH) (Ezek 23:12)

סֶרֶן   lord; ruler; chief (SDBH) (Josh 13:3)

עַתּוּד   leader (SDBH); leader, male goat (DCH) (Isa 14:9)

פֶּחָה   prefect, governor (Neh 5:14)

פָּלִיל   magistrate, judge (Deut 32:31 R)

פֶּרֶז   chief; leader; commander (SDBH); warrior, ruler (DCH) (Hab 3:14 H)

קָצִין   ruler, leader (Josh 10:24)

רֹאשׁ   head, leader, ruler (Josh 11:10)

רוֹזֵן   ruler (Ps 2:2 R)

שַׂר   head person, chieftain, general, prince (Num 31:14)

Foreign Rulers and Leaders

אֲחַשְׁדַּרְפַּן satrap, governor (Persian) (Esth 3:12 R)

מֶלְצַר royal guardian (Persian) (Dan 1:16 R)

פַּרְעֹה Pharaoh (SDBH) (Gen 12:15)

שַׁרְבִיט scepter (Persian) (Esth 4:11 R)

תִּרְשָׁתָא governor (Persian) (SDBH) (Neh 7:65 R)

Royal Ornament: Scepters/Staffs/Crowns/Throne/Footstool

אֶצְעָדָה royal armlet (Salvesen "The Trappings") (2 Sam 1:10 R)

הֲדֹם footstool (Salvesen "The Trappings") (Isa 66:1 R)

כִּסֵּא throne (Salvesen "The Trappings") (1 Kgs 10:9)

כֶּתֶר royal crown (Salvesen "The Trappings") (Esth 1:11 R)

מְחֹקֵק ruler's staff; commander, sceptre (DCH) (Gen 49:10 R)

מַטֶּה rod; tribe; branch (Ps 110:2)

מַקֵּל staff, rod; branch (Jer 48:17)

מִשְׁעֶנֶת staff, support, symbol of authority (כלי) (Num 21:18)

נֵזֶר crown, royal and priestly headgear (Salvesen "The Trappings"); consecration, crown, diadem (DCH) (Ps 89:40)

פַּךְ שֶׁמֶן anointing horn, anointing flask (to anoint kings) (Pritz) (1 Sam 10:1)

עֲטָרָה crown (Salvesen "The Trappings"); garland wreath (Salvesen "עֲטָרָה") (Ezek 21:31)

קֶרֶן anointing horn, anointing flask (to anoint kings) (Pritz) (1 Sam 16:1)

שֵׁבֶט rod, staff; clan, tribe (כלי, Salvesen, "שֵׁבֶט") (Ps 45:7)

שַׁרְבִיט scepter, stick (Esth 4:11)

Government: Administration

אָצִיל leader (SDBH) (Exod 24:11 H)

אַשָּׁף conjurer; enchanter; exorcist; sorcerer (SDBH) (Dan 1:20 R)

גִּזְבָּר treasurer (Hurvitz) (Ezra 1:8 H)

דַּיָּן judge, advocate (1 Sam 24:16)

חָכָם wise, teacher, sage; learned man, scholar (Van der Toorn) (Prov 1:6)

חַרְטֹם magician, diviner (at royal court) (SDBH) (Gen 41:8)

טַבָּחָה/טַבָּח guard; butcher; cook (SDBH) (1 Sam 8:13)

טִפְסָר commander; officer; official; overseer; scribe (SDBH) (Jer 51:27 R)

מַזְכִּיר recorder; chronicler (SDBH); scribe (DCH) (2 Sam 8:16)

מַסְגֵּר women of the harem (DCH) (Jer 24:1 H)

מַשְׁקֶה cup-bearer, royal butler (Gen 40:13)

סֹפֵר scribe (Jer 8:8)

סָרִיס government official, eunuch (foreign) (Esth 1:10)

עֶבֶד slave; servant; officer; official; subject; vassal (SDBH) (Gen 9:25)

פָּקִיד superintendent, overseer (Jer 20:1)

שֹׁטֵר scribe, official, magistrate; military officer (Deut 1:15)

שֹׁפֵט judge; tribal military leader (Ps 94:2)

שָׂרֵי הָרְכוּשׁ royal overseers (of estates) (Borowski *Agriculture*) (1 Chr 27:31)

Artisans

אָמָּן / אָמוֹן skilled worker; artisan (SDBH) (Song 7:2 H)

אֹרֵג weaver (Isa 19:9)

בָּחוֹן tester; assayer (SDBH) (Jer 6:27 H)

גַּלָּב barber (SDBH) (Ezek 5:1 H)

חֹקֵק engraver, carver; commander (DCH) (Judg 5:9)

חָרָשׁ / חָרֵשׁ artisan, craftsman, blacksmith (Exod 28:11)

חֹשֵׁב inventor; designer (SDBH) (Exod 26:1)

יוֹצֵר potter, artisan, sculptor (Isa 41:25)

מְכַבֵּס launderer, cleaner, fuller (Mal 3:2)

מַסְגֵּר locksmith; smith, metalworker (DCH) (Jer 29:2 R)

מַצְרֵף refiner, crucible (for silver); crucible (Guillame, DCH) (Prov 17:3 R)

צוֹרֵף smelter, smith (gold, silver); metal smelter, refiner (DCH) (Isa 40:19)

צָרוֹף metal smelter, refiner (DCH) (Jer 6:29 H)

רַקָּחָה / רַקָּח perfumer (1 Sam 8:13 H)

רֹקֵם embroiderer (SDBH) (Exod 26:36 R)

Merchants/Business/Banking

כֶּסֶף silver, money (1 Chr 29:2)

לֹוֶה borrower (Prov 19:17)

מוֹכֵר seller (Neh 13:20)

מַכָּר business accessor, temple official valuing sacrifices (DCH) (2 Kgs 12:6 R)

מִקְנָה price; acquisition (Gen 17:12)

נֹשֶׁה lender, userer (2 Kgs 4:1)

נֶשֶׁךְ interest, usury (Exod 22:24)

סֹחֵר trader, merchant (Isa 23:8)

סַחַר profit, merchandise, mart, trade (Isa 23:18 R)

קֹנֶה / קוֹנֶה buyer (Ezek 7:12)

קִנְיָן purchase (Gen 36:6)

קְשִׂיטָה money, weight; kesitah, weight of silver or gold (DCH)
(Job 42:11 R)

רֹוכֵל trader, merchant (Ezek 27:3)

רְכֻלָּה merchandise, stock; trade (DCH) (Ezek 28:5 R)

שָׂכָר wages, payment (Jonah 1:3)

Food Production

אִכָּר farmer, plowman (Joel 1:11)

אֹפֶה baker (Gen 40:1)

בֹּוקֵר herdsman; cattle breeder (SDBH) (Amos 7:14 H)

בֹּולֵס person who tends sycamore trees for a living (SDBH); fig tender (DCH) (Amos 7:14 H)

בעה to boil (Peters) (Isa 64:1 R)

בשל to boil (Peters) (Joel 4:13)

דֻּוג / דָּיָג fisherman (Isa 19:8 R)

זיד to boil, to stew (Peters) (Gen 25:29)

זֹרֵעַ sower (Borowski *Agriculture*) (Isa 55:10)

לבב to create (Peters), to bake (DCH) (2 Sam 13:6 R)

מֹשֵׁךְ הַזָּרַע sower (poetic) (Borowski *Agriculture*) (Amos 9:13)

נֹקֵד herdsmen (Steiner); sheep breeder (DCH) (Amos 1:1 R)

עוג to create (Peters), to bake (DCH) (Ezek 4:12 H)

צַיָּד hunter (Jer 16:16 H)

צלה to boil (DCH), to apply dry heat (Peters) (Isa 44:19 R)

קלה to roast (DCH), to apply dry heat (Peters) (Josh 5:11 R)

רֹעֶה shepherd (Ps 23:1)

רֹעֶה shepherd (Isa 38:12 R)

רתח to boil (DCH), to create turbulence with heat (Peters) (Ezek 24:5 R)

Prostitute/Sex Worker

זֹנָה prostitute, sex worker (Gen 34:31)

כֶּלֶב male shrine prostitute, "dog" (epithet) (SDBH) (Deut 23:19 R)

מַסְגֵּר women of the harem (DCH) (Jer 24:1 H)

קָדֵשׁ male temple prostitute (SDBH) (Deut 23:18 R)

קְדֵשָׁה sacred prostitute, female devotee (Gen 38:21 R)

MILITARY

War: General Terms

חֵרֶם	ban, total destruction (1 Kgs 20:42)
הֵידָד	shout, war-cry (Jer 51:14 R)
לָחָם	battle, war; warrior (DCH) (Judg 5:8 H)
מִלְחָמָה	war (Num 31:27)
מָצוֹר	siege; siege wall (Pritz) (Deut 20:20 R)
קְרָב	battle, war, hostile encounter (Ps 55:22 R)
שׁוֹפָר	ram's horn (blown to summon forces) (ELT) (Judg 3:27)
תְּרוּעָה	war-cry, alarm (of trumpets) (Num 23:21)

Enemy/Victory/Defeat

אֹיֵב	adversary, enemy (Num 10:9)
בַּז	plunder (Ezek 34:28)
גְּבוּרָה	force, victory, valor; might (DCH) (Isa 30:15)
יָרִיב	adversary, enemy (SDBH) (Ps 35:1 R)
יְשׁוּעָה	deliverance, victory, salvation (Isa 33:2)
מַגֵּפָה	slaughter, defeat, plague (Ezek 24:16)
עָר	foe, enemy (1 Sam 28:16 R)
צַר	enemy (Num 24:8)
קִים	enemy, adversary, opponent (SDBH); rebellion (DCH) (Job 22:20 H)
שׁוּר	foe, oppressor; watcher (DCH) (Ps 92:12 H)
שׁוֹרֵר	enemy (SDBH) (Ps 5:9 R)
שָׂטָן	opponent; adversary, Satan (DCH) (Num 22:22)

Army

אַלְקוּם	levy, band of soldiers (Prov 30:31 H)
חַיִל	army, force; outer wall, outer fortification (SDBH); rampart (DCH) (2 Sam 20:15)
עִזּוּז	an army; forcible; mighty (DCH) (Ps 24:8 R)
עַם	army; people, nation (Gen 11:6)
צָבָא	army; assembly, group, division (DCH) (Exod 6:26)

Officers/Leaders

טִפְסָר	military governor; commander, officer, official, overseer, scribe, recruiting officer (SDBH) (Jer 51:27 R)
נָגִיד	commander (Ps 76:13)
נְצִיב	governor (SDBH) (1 Kgs 4:19)
סָגָן	official, prefect (Jer 51:57)

סֶרֶן   lord, ruler, tyrant (Judg 16:5)

פֶּחָה   governor (1 Kgs 10:15)

שֹׁטֵר / שׁוֹטֵר   officer, foreman, supervisor (SDBH) (Exod 5:6)

שַׁלִּיט   prince, warrior; subordinate officer (DCH) (Gen 42:6)

שָׁלִישׁ   adjutant, general of the third rank; third man, officer (DCH) (1 Kgs 9:22)

שַׂר   head, leader; commanders of various ranks within the army (Seevers) (1 Sam 22:7)

תַּרְתָּן   commander-in-chief, person with an extremely high position in the Assyrian kingdom (SDBH); Tartan (title) (DCH) (2 Kgs 18:17 R)

Soldiers

אִישׁ הַבֵּנַיִם   "man of the interval," champion (in reference to Goliath) (SDBH, DCH) (1 Sam 17:4)

אֶלֶף   thousand, clan, division in army (Seevers) (1 Sam 23:23)

אֶרְאֵל / אֲרִיאֵל   mighty warrior (SDBH) (Isa 33:7 R)

גִּבּוֹר   hero, warrior (Gen 10:8)

גֶּבֶר   warrior, valiant man; man (DCH) (Job 38:3)

גְּדוּד   band of raiders; troops (SDBH) (Gen 49:19)

גַּמָּדִים   brave man, brave soldier (Ezek 27:11 H)

טַבָּח   guard; butcher; guard, bodyguard (SDBH) (Gen 37:36)

יוֹרֶה   archer (SDBH) (1 Chr 10:3)

מוֹרֶה   archer (SDBH) (1 Sam 31:3)

מִשְׁמָר   a guard; watch, lookout (Ezek 38:7)

נְצִיב   garrison (SDBH) (1 Sam 10:5)

נֹשֵׂא כֵלִים   equipment bearer (for an important soldier) (Seevers) (Judg 9:54)

סֹאֵן   soldier, warrior (shod) (Isa 9:4 H)

עֹזֵר   warrior, hero; helper (DCH) (Ps 30:11)

פְּקוּדִים   mustered soldiers, troops; precepts (DCH) (Num 14:29)

פָּרָשׁ   horseman, (plural) cavalry (SDBH) (Gen 50:9)

צָבָא   soldier fit for war (SDBH); host (DCH) (Num 1:3)

קַלָּע   slinger (DCH) (2 Kgs 3:25 H)

רַגְלִי   footman, infantry; on foot (DCH) (1 Kgs 20:29)

Weapons/Armor

General Arms

חֵצֶן   weapons, arms; war-horses (DCH) (Ezek 23:24 H)

כְּלִי   weapon (Gen 49:5)

מְכֵרָה   weapon, staff (DCH) (Gen 49:5 H)

מֶשֶׁק arms, military equipment, arsenal; acquisition, possession (DCH) (Gen 15:2 H)

נֶשֶׁק/נֵשֶׁק armor, weapons (2 Kgs 10:2)

שׁוֹט whip (SDBH) (1 Kgs 12:11)

שֶׁלַח weapon; missile, shoot (DCH) (Neh 4:17 R)

תְּלִי weapon; quiver ("hang") (Gen 27:3 H)

Armor

דֶּבֶק joint, appendage of armor (Hobbs, DCH) (1 Kgs 22:34 R)

מָעוֹז רֹאשׁ helmet (Pritz) (Ps 60:9)

מִצְחָה greaves (1 Sam 17:6 H)

סְאוֹן military boot (Isa 9:4 H)

קוֹבַע/כּוֹבַע helmet (Ezek 23:24 R)

קַשְׂקֶשֶׂת scale, coat of mail (1 Sam 17:5 R)

שִׁרְיָה coat of mail; arrow; javelin (SDBH) (Job 41:18 H)

שִׁרְיוֹן/סִרְיוֹן coat of mail; breastplate, scale armor (Pritz); chest protector (SDBH) (1 Sam 17:5)

תַּחֲרָא coat of mail (Exod 28:32 R)

Shields

מָגֵן shield; small shield (Pritz) (2 Sam 22:3)

סֹכֵךְ moveable shield, mantelet (Pritz) (Nah 2:6 H)

עֲגִלוֹת small shields (Ps 46:10 H)

צִנָּה large shield; buckler; hook; thorn (1 Sam 17:7)

שֶׁלֶט shield; quiver (?); small shield, buckler (Pritz) (2 Sam 8:7 R)

Swords and Sheaths

אִבְחָה brandishing (sword) (Ezek 21:20 H)

בָּרָק lightning; flashing sword (Ps 18:15)

חֶרֶב sword, knife, dagger; butchers' knives, swords, razors; curved sword (Koller) (Gen 34:26)

מְכֵרֹת swords (Pritz); weapons (DCH) (Gen 49:5 H)

נָדָן sheath (1 Chr 21:27 H)

פְּתָחָה drawn sword (Ps 55:22)

תַּעַר scabbard, sheath; razor (Koller) (1 Sam 17:51 R)

Club/Axe

מַפֵּץ smiter, war club; hammer, club (Hobbs) (Jer 51:20)

מַקֵּל יָד club, war club, mace (Pritz) (Ezek 39:9)

סְגֹר battle-axe (Pritz) (Ps 35:3 H)

תּוֹתָח club, war club, mace (Pritz) (Job 41:21 H)

Sling

אֶבֶן stone (1 Sam 17:40)

מַרְגֵּמָה sling (Pritz) (Prov 26:8 H)

קֶלַע sling (Judg 20:16 R)

Bow and Arrow

אַשְׁפָּה arrow-case, quiver (Job 39:23 R)

בֶּן־קָשֶׁת arrow (Pritz) (Job 41:20)

בְּנֵי אַשְׁפָּה arrow (Pritz) (Lam 3:13)

זֵק flaming arrow; spark, brand; fiery missile (כְּלִי)
(Prov 26:18 R)

חֵץ / חֵצִי arrow, shaft of spear (Gen 49:23 R)

יֶתֶר bowstring (Pritz); cord, bow string, tent ropes, sinews (DCH)
(Judg 16:7 R)

מַטֶּה arrow (Pritz); staff, scepter, shaft of arrow, stem of vine
(DCH) (Hab 3:9)

מֵיתָר bowstring (Pritz); cord (DCH) (Ps 21:12 R)

רֶשֶׁף arrow (Pritz) (Ps 76:3 R)

קֶשֶׁת / קֹשֶׁט bow (Gen 21:16)

רַב / רׇב archer (Pritz) (Job 16:13 R)

רבב shoot an arrow (Gen 49:23 R)

רְבָבוֹת shafts of arrows (Ps 3:7 H)

שֶׁלֶט quiver (?); small shield, buckler (Pritz) (Jer 51:11 R)

תְּלִי quiver (Pritz) (Gen 27:3 H)

Lance/Spear/Missile

חֲנִית javelin, lance (1 Sam 13:19)

כִּידוֹן knife, dart, javelin, scimitar; long straight sword, carried only
by foreigners (Koller) (Josh 8:18 R)

לֶהָבָה spearhead (Pritz) (1 Sam 17:7)

מַסָּע missile, dart, quarry (1 Kgs 6:7 R)

קַיִן spearhead (Pritz); spear, lance (DCH) (2 Sam 21:16 H)

רֹמַח lance, iron point, spear ("throw"); spear (SDBH)
(Num 25:7)

שֵׁבֶט spear, lance (Pritz); rod, staff, lance (DCH) (2 Sam 18:14)

שֶׁלַח spear, missile; branch; weapon (SDBH) (Joel 2:8 R)

שִׁרְיָה javelin (Pritz) (Job 41:18 H)

Battering Ram

חֲרָבוֹת battering rams (Pritz); swords (DCH) (Ezek 26:9)

חִשְּׁבֹנוֹת catapult, ballista (Pritz); war engine (DCH)
(2 Chr 26:15 R)

כַּר battering ram; camel's saddle; elaborate ladies' saddle (כְּלִי)
(Ezek 4:2)

קֹבֶל siege-engine; battering ram (SDBH) (Ezek 26:9 H)

Vehicles, Horses, and Travel

Chariots

גַּלְגַּל/גִּלְגָּל   wheel (Isa 5:28); wheel, cart, wagon, chariot (SDBH, Pritz) (Ezek 23:24)

אוֹפָן   wheel (Exod 14:25)

אַפִּרְיוֹן   palanquin, litter (SDBH) (Song 3:9 H)

אֹרַח   caravan, path, way (DCH) (Judg 5:6)

גַּב   wheel rim (Pritz) (1 Kgs 7:33)

חִשֻּׁק   wheel-spoke, rod (1 Kgs 7:33 H)

חִשֻּׁר   hub of wheel (1 Kgs 7:33 H)

יָד   axle of wheel (Pritz) (1 Kgs 7:32)

מֶרְכָּבָה   chariot (Gen 41:43)

סֶרֶן   axle of wheel (Pritz) (1 Kgs 7:30 H)

עֲגָלָה   cart, wagon (Gen 45:19)

פָּרָשׁ   cavalry, horse (Jer 4:29)

צַב   covered wagon, litter (Num 7:3 R)

רַכָּב   charioteer (1 Kgs 22:34 R)

רֶכֶב   chariotry; chariot, charioteers (DCH) (Gen 50:9)

רִכְבָּה   riding, driving (Ezek 27:20 H)

רְכוּב   vehicle (Ps 104:3)

Road

אֹרַח   way, path; caravan, traveller (Gen 49:17)

דֶּרֶךְ   road, way (Gen 24:27)

הֵלֶךְ   journey; traveller (1 Sam 14:26 R)

חוּץ   street, road (Pritz) (Josh 2:19)

מְסִלָּה   highway, path (Num 20:19)

מַסְלוּל   highway (Pritz); gatehouse, gateway (DCH) (Isa 35:8 R)

מַסַּע   setting out, station, stage, journey (Num 33:2)

מַעְגָּל   wagon track, path; moral path (poetic) (Aitken "מַעְגָּל") (Ps 17:5)

מִשְׁעוֹל   road, street (Pritz); pathway within vineyard (Aitken "מִשְׁעוֹל") (Num 22:24 H)

נֵס   sign, banner, pole; standard, ensign (DCH) (Isa 5:26)

נָתִיב   path; traveller (Judg 5:6 R)

פֶּגֶר   monument, memorial (SDBH); memorial stele (DCH) (Ezek 43:7 R)

צִיּוּן   guidepost, marker, sign, monument, road pillar (2 Kgs 23:17 R)

שָׁבִיל   way (Jer 18:15 R)

שׁוּק   street, road (Pritz) (Prov 7:8 R)

תַּמְרוּר pillar, road marker (Jer 31:21 H)

Formations/Groups

אֲגַף/אֲגַפִּים forces, wings of an army; band, crowd of troops (Ezek 38:6 R)

גְּדוּד troop (1 Chr 7:4)

חָמֵשׁ battle array (five) (Num 31:32)

מַעֲרָכָה military array (1 Sam 17:21)

מַצָּבָה military guard (1 Sam 14:12 H)

Flags/Standards

אוֹת sign; standards, ensigns (Num 2:2)

דֶּגֶל banners, standards; division (Num 1:52)

נֵס standard, ensign, banner (Pritz) (Isa 5:26)

תֹּרֶן standard, ensign, banner (Pritz); mast, flag, pole (DCH) (Isa 30:17 R)

Fortifications

Fortress

אֲגַם fortress (SDBH); pool, swamp (DCH) (Jer 51:32 R)

אַרְמוֹן citadel (1 Kgs 16:18)

בִּירָה fortress, castle, palace (2 Chr 17:12)

בִּצָּרוֹן fortress, castle (Zech 9:12 H)

טִירָה fortress, hamlet, encampment, wall (Song 8:9 R)

מִבְצָר fortification, castle, fortified city (2 Sam 24:7)

מַחֲנֶה encampment (Judg 7:9)

מִלּוֹא citadel, rampart (1 Kgs 9:15 R)

מִסְגֶּרֶת fortress, stronghold (Pritz) (2 Sam 22:46)

מָעוֹז fortified place, defense (Isa 23:11)

מְצָד/מְצוּדָה fort, mountain, fortress, stronghold (2 Sam 5:7)

מָצוֹר/מְצוּרָה mound, rampart, fortification (2 Chr 11:10 R); watchtower, tower (Hab 2:1 R) (Pritz)

מִשְׂגָּב high fort, defense, tower (2 Sam 22:3)

עֹפֶל mound, fortress (Mic 4:8 R)

Wall

חוֹמָה wall (Deut 28:52)

חִיצוֹן exterior (of wall) (2 Kgs 16:18)

חָרוּץ moat (Pritz) (Dan 9:25 H)

כֹּתֶל wall (of house) (Song 2:9 H)

מַעֲקֶה parapet (top of wall) (Deut 22:8 H)

קִיר city wall; side (2 Kgs 4:10)

שׁוּר wall (of rich house) (Gen 49:22 R)

שָׁרָה fortification wall (Jer 5:10 H)

תָּא guardroom (Pritz) (1 Kgs 14:28)

Armory, Arsenal

אוֹצָר armory, arsenal (Pritz) (Jer 50:25)

בֵּית כְּלִי armory, arsenal (Pritz) (2 Kgs 20:13)

נֶשֶׁק/נֵשֶׁק armory, arsenal (Pritz) (Neh 3:19)

Tower

אַלְמָנוֹת watchtowers (Pritz); widows (DCH) (Isa 13:22 R)

אַשְׁיָה bulwark, tower, bastion (SDBH) (Jer 50:15 H)

פִּנָּה watchtower, tower (Pritz) (Zeph 1:16)

מִגְדָּל tower (Judg 8:9)

מָצוֹר tower, fortress, refuge (2 Chr 11:10)

מִצְפֶּה watchtower, tower (Pritz) (Isa 21:8 R)

שֶׁמֶשׁ watchtower, tower (Pritz) (Isa 54:12 H)

Siege

אֹרַח embarkment, earthwork for siege (DCH) (Job 30:12 H)

בַּחַן/בָּחוּן siege tower, watchtower (Isa 32:14 R)

דָּיֵק siege wall (2 Kgs 25:1 R)

מָצָב firing platform, siege tower (Pritz) (Isa 29:3 H)

מָצוֹד siege wall (Pritz) (Eccl 9:14 R)

מְצוּרָה firing platforms, siege towers (Pritz); fortification, fortress (DCH) (Isa 29:3)

סֹלְלָה siege-ramp, siege-mound (2 Sam 20:15)

Bunker

חֵיל entrenchment, rampart, tower (?), fortress (2 Sam 20:15)

צְרִיחַ bunker, underground room; watchtower (?) (Judg 9:46 R)

Post/Outpost

מִצְפֶּה observatory, post; watchtower (DCH) (Isa 21:8 R)

נְצִיב military post, garrison; sentry (1 Sam 10:5)

Spoils, Plunder, Booty

בַּז spoils, plunder (captives, cattle); prey (Ezek 34:28)

בִּזָּה prey, spoils (Dan 11:24)

גֶּזֶל robbery; plundered goods (Ezek 22:29 R)

גְּזֵלָה seized goods, stolen goods (Isa 3:14 R)

חֲלִיצָה stripped off (spoils, armour) (Judg 14:19 R)

מֶכֶס tribute, tax (Num 31:37 R)

מַלְקוֹחַ booty (cattle, captives); prey; plunder (DCH) (Num 31:12 R)

מְשִׁסָּה spoils, prey, booty (Isa 42:22 R)

עַד booty (Zeph 3:8 R)

שָׁלָל plunder, booty (Josh 22:8)

Captive/Exile

אָסִיר/אַסִּיר captive, bound; prisoner (DCH) (Job 3:18)

גוֹלָה exile, exiles (Isa 49:21)

גָּלוּת captivity, exile; diaspora (DCH) (Isa 20:4)

שְׁבוּת exile; prosperity (Deut 30:3)

שְׁבִי captives, captivity (Ezra 2:1)

שִׁבְיָה captivity, captives (2 Chr 28:5 R)

שׁוֹלָל prisoner, captive; nude; barefoot, led in fetters (DCH)
(Job 12:19 R)

Chains/Bonds/Fetters

אֲזִקִּים chains, bonds, manacles (Jer 40:1 R)

אֵסוּר bond, manacle (Judg 15:14)

חַרְצֻבָּה bands; grief (Isa 58:6 R)

כֶּבֶל fetter (Ps 105:18 R)

מוֹסֵר fetter, bond (Job 39:5 R)

MARITIME
Ships

אֳנִי	fleet, ships, navy (1 Kgs 9:26 R)
אֳנִי־שַׁיִט	galley, lit. "rowing ship" (Patai) (Isa 33:21)
אֳנִיָּה	ship (Gen 49:13)
אֳנִיּוֹת אֵבֶה	reed ships (Patai); papyrus ship (DCH) (Job 9:26)
אֳנִיּוֹת תַּרְשִׁישׁ	Tarshish ships, large seagoing vessels (Patai) (1 Kgs 22:49)
דֹּבְרוֹת	rafts; floats (SDBH) (1 Kgs 5:23 H)
כְּלִי־גֹמֶא	"vessels of papyrus" (Patai) (Isa 18:2)
סְפִינָה	ship (SDBH) (Jonah 1:5 H)
עֲבָרָה	ferry boat (Patai) (2 Sam 19:19 H)
צִי	ship (Dan 11:30 R)
צִי אַדִּיר	large ship (Patai) (Isa 33:21)
רַפְסֹדֹת	rafts (2 Chr 2:15 H)
שְׂכִיָּה	ship (Isa 2:16 H)
תֵּבָה	basket; ark (SDBH); e.g., Noah's ark; chest, ark (Patai) (Gen 6:14)

Crew

אַנְשֵׁי אֳנִיּוֹת	crew, literally "men of the ship" (Patai) (1 Kgs 9:27)
חֹבֵל	sailor ("handles rope") (Jonah 1:6 R)
יֹדְעֵי הַיָּם	crew, literally "knowers of the sea" (Patai) (1 Kgs 9:27)
מַלָּח	seaman, sailor, mariner (Ezek 27:27 R)
רַב הַחֹבֵל	captain of the ship, literally "master roper" (Patai) (Jonah 1:6)
שָׁטִים	rowers, oarsmen (Patai) (Ezek 27:26)
תֹּפְשֵׂי מָשׁוֹט	oar holders, oarsmen (Patai) (Ezek 27:29)

Structures

חֶבֶל	cable, rope; mast (Pritz); perhaps tackle rigging (DCH) (Prov 23:34 H)
חֵבֶל	rope, cord holding sail in place (Patai) (Isa 33:23)
חוֹמוֹת	sides of a hull (Patai) (Ezek 27:11)
כֵּן	socket for mast (Patai) (Isa 33:23)
כֹּפֶר	pitch, bitumen (for sealing ship hull) (Patai) (Gen 6:14 H)
לוּחַ	plank, board (Ezek 27:5)
מִפְרָשׂ	sail (spread out) (Ezek 27:7 R)
מָשׁוֹט / מִשּׁוֹט	rudder, oar (Ezek 27:6 R)
נֵס	ensign, standard; sail; yard, ensign (Patai); sail (Pritz) (Isa 33:23)
קֶרֶשׁ	deck, room, mast (Ezek 27:6)

רֹאשׁ חִבֵּל   top of the mast (Patai) (Prov 23:34)
שׁוֹט   to row (Ezek 27:8)
שַׁיִט   oar (Pritz) (Isa 33:21 H)
תַּחְתִּים   lower decks (DCH) (Gen 6:16)
תֹּרֶן   mast; flagstaff (SDBH) (Isa 30:17 R)

Trade/Cargo

מַעֲרָב   merchandise, goods (Ezek 27:27 R)
עִזָּבוֹן   wares, merchandise (Ezek 27:12 R)
ערב   to conduct trade (Ezek 27:9 R)

MUSIC

General Terms and Types

גִּתִּית musical term, meaning unknown; possibly associated with the winepress or with the town of Gath (SBDH); in psalm titles, "perhaps an instrument or melody associated with (musician from) Gath or with winepress" (DCH) (Ps 8:1 R)

זָמִיר song (Isa 25:5 R)

זִמְרָה music, melody, song (Exod 15:2 R)

מִזְמוֹר music, poem, psalm (Ps 30:1)

מַנְגִּינָה mocking song (Lam 3:63 H)

מְנַגֵּן musician (2 Kgs 3:15)

נֹגְנִים / נְגִינוֹת musicians; possibly a string instrument (Kolyada) (Ps 68:26)

סֶלָה pause (Ps 3:3)

עֲלָמוֹת / עַלְמוּת ambiguous technical notation: high key/register, falsetto (1 Chr 15:20) (Burgh); perhaps sotto voce as musical term (DCH) (Ps 9:1 H)

קַו sound, music, melody, rhythm (DCH) (Ps 19:5)

עֹז poetic and musical performance (DCH) (2 Sam 6:14 R)

עָנָה to sing; utter a shout (DCH) (Isa 13:22)

קִינָה dirge, funeral song; lamentation (2 Chr 35:25)

שִׁיר song, singing (Ps 65:1)

שְׁמִינִת "according to the Sheminith" in Psalm titles, perhaps for psalms played on instrument with eight strings or in the eighth key (DCH); low key/register (Burgh); the eighth (Smith) (Ps 6:1)

שָׁרִים singers (Ps 68:26)

תְּהִלָּה laudation, hymn; psalm, praise, adoration (DCH) (Isa 42:8)

תְּפִלָּה hymn, intersession, supplication (2 Sam 7:27)

Instruments

Flute

חָלַל play the pipe (1 Kgs 1:40)

חָלִיל flute, pipe; double-reed woodwind instrument (Kolyada); clarinet, oboe (Braun); pipe (Montagu); double pipe (Mitchell); double pipe (Burgh); double reed pipe (Smith) (Isa 5:12 R)

נְחִילוֹת lamentation pipes (Borowski *Daily Life*); flutes (DCH) (Ps 5:1 H)

עוּגָב flute, reed instrument; lute (Borowski *Daily Life*), generic woodwind term (Montagu); pipe, flute (DCH) (Ps 150:4 R)

String

כִּנּוֹר	harp, lyre; generic term for all stringed instruments or a specific stringed instrument (Kolyada) (Isa 5:12)
מֶן	string (of instrument) (Ps 45:9)
מִנִּים	stringed instruments (Braun) (Ps 150:4 H)
נֵבֶל / נֶבֶל	harp, lyre; skin-bag; possibly a bass lyre (Kolyada); a large כִּנּוֹר (Borowski *Daily Life*) (Isa 5:12)
נְגִינָה	stringed instrument; poem; string music, mocking song (DCH) (Ps 69:13)
נגן	to play (a stringed instrument); to accompany song with a stringed instrument (DCH) (1 Sam 16:16)
עָשׂוֹר	ten-stringed harp (Ps 92:4)
שְׁמִינִית	eight-stringed harp; "according to the Sheminith" in Psalm titles, perhaps for psalms played on instrument with eight strings or in the eighth key (DCH); low key/register (Burgh); the eighth (Smith) (Ps 6:1)

Horn

חֲצוֹצְרָה / חֲצֹצְרָה	trumpet, straight trumpet made of metal (Kolyada); trumpet made of silver (Braun) (Ps 98:6)
יוֹבֵל	horn, ram's horn, trumpet; jubilee horn (Kolyada) (Exod 19:13)
קֶרֶן	bull horn, ox horn (Kolyada); symbol of strength, might, pride (DCH); ram's horn (Braun) (Josh 6:5)
שׁוֹפָר	curved horn, ram's horn; trumpet (DCH) (Josh 6:16)
תָּקוֹעַ	trumpet; horn (sounded for battle) (DCH) (Ezek 7:14 H)
תֶּקַע	blast (of ram's horn) (DCH) (Ps 150:3 H)
תְּרוּעָה	trumpet blast, battle cry, loud noise (Num 23:21)

Cymbals, Shakers, Bells

מִלְחָמָה	adaptation, harmony, sistrum (DCH) (Isa 30:32 H)
מְנַעַנְעִים	sistrum (Mitchell); clay rattle (Braun); rattles (Burgh) (2 Sam 6:5 H)
מְצִלָּה	bell, tinkler; small bell on horses (HALOT) (Zech 14:20 H)
מְצִלְתַּיִם / מְצִלּוֹת	pair of cymbals (Kolyada) (Zech 14:20)
עֲצֵי בְרוֹשִׁים	cypress wood clappers (Smith) (2 Sam 6:5)
פַּעֲמֹן / פַּעֲמוֹן	bell; bell on high priest's robe (DCH) (Exod 28:34 R)
צְלָצַל	cymbal; whirring; insect; sistrums (Borowski *Daily Life*) (Ps 150:5 R)
שָׁלִשִׁים	sistrum (Kolyada); rattle (Montagu); sistrum (Smith) (1 Sam 18:6 H)
תֹּף	tambourine; timbrel (DCH); frame drum (Burgh); small, round, hand-held frame drum (Smith) (Ps 81:3)

Dance

חֹלְלִים dancers (root חוּל) (Ps 87:7) (Smith); flautists (root חלל) (1 Kgs 1:40) (DCH)

מָחוֹל dance, dancing, circle dance (Lam 5:15 R)

מְכַרְכֵּר leaping and whirling about (of David) (Montagu) (2 Sam 6:14 R)

שׂחק to dance, play (an instrument) (Smith); play (games), entertain (DCH) (2 Sam 6:5)

EDUCATION

Teachers and Students

בֵּית מִדְרָשׁ   school (Van der Toorn) (not used in Hebrew Bible; see Sir 51:23)

דַּעַת   knowledge (Widder) (Isa 40:14)

חָכָם   wise, teacher, sage; learned man, scholar (Van der Toorn) (Prov 1:6)

חָכְמָה   wisdom, prudence (including in religious matters) (Van der Toorn) (Deut 4:6)

לִמֻּד   pupil, apprentice, student; thing taught, teaching (DCH); instruction (Widder) (Isa 8:16 R)

לֶקַח   learning, teaching (Deut 32:2 R)

מַדָּע   knowledge, thought (Hurvitz) (Eccl 10:20 R)

מִדְרָשׁ   written composition, study/exegesis of a written (sacred) text (Hurvitz) (2 Chr 13:22 H)

מוֹדִיעִים   religious officials (Widder); astrologers (DCH) (Isa 47:13 R)

מוּסָר   instruction in behavior, discipline, punishment (Widder) (Prov 1:8)

מְלַמֵּד   teacher (Widder) (Ps 119:99 R)

מוֹרֶה   teacher, priestly teacher (Widder) (Isa 30:20 R)

סֹפֵר   scribe, scholar of texts (Van der Toorn) (2 Chr 34:13)

תּוֹרָה   Torah, parental instruction, priestly instruction (Widder) (Jer 18:18)

תַּלְמִיד   student, apprentice (Hurvitz); scholar (DCH) (1 Chr 25:8 H)

Writing Tools and Implements

(For Writing on Paper/Stone, see Tools ➡ Artisanal Tools ➡ Carving/Writing)

אִגֶּרֶת   letter, missive, epistle, royal letter, edict (Hurvitz) (Neh 2:7)

גִּלָּיוֹן   blank scroll (Zhakevich); tablet for writing on (DCH) (Isa 8:1 H)

דְּיוֹ   ink (Zhakevich) (Jer 36:18 H)

דֶּלֶת   door, column, writing board (Zhakevich); column of writing in a scroll (כלי) (Jer 36:23 H)

חֶרֶשׂ   potsherd (Zhakevich) (Isa 30:14)

כְּתָב   document, letter, edict, writing (DCH) (Esth 1:22)

לוּחַ   tablet (Notebaart); tablet, board, plank (Zhakevich) (Isa 30:8)

מְגִלָּה   scroll made of papyrus or leather (Zhakevich) (Jer 36:23)

מְגִלַּת־סֵפֶר   scroll document (Zhakevich) (Ezek 2:9)

מִכְתָּב   writing, script, document, inscription (DCH) (Exod 39:30 R)

נִשְׁתְּוָן   official letter (Persian) (כלי) (Ezra 4:7 R)

סֵפֶר scroll (Notebaart); document, record, book, register, epistle, literature (DCH) (Isa 30:8)

סְפֹרָה document, scroll, learning (DCH) (Ps 56:9 H)

סְפֹרָה literacy, art of writing (DCH) (Ps 71:15 H)

עוֹר skin of human or animal, perhaps used for vellum (Zhakevich) (Lev 8:17)

קֶסֶת cup, ink well; scribal palette (Zhakevich); writing case (DCH) (Ezek 9:2 R)

תַּעַר הַסֹּפֵר scribal knife, scribal razor (Zhakevich, Koller) (Jer 36:23)

PART IV

THE CONSTRUCTED ORDER

BUILDINGS AND STRUCTURES

Town and Village

חַוָּה settlement (SDBH); tent village (DCH) (Num 32:41 R)

חֵיל town (SDBH) (1 Kgs 21:23 R)

חָצֵר village, settlement (SDBH) (Gen 25:16)

טִירָה camp, encampment, village (SDBH) (Gen 25:16 R)

מְדִינָה province, district (Esth 1:1)

עִיר city; town (SDBH) (Gen 4:17)

פְּרָזוֹת unwalled towns, villages (SDBH) (Ezek 38:11)

קֶרֶת city, town (SDBH) (Job 29:7 R)

רְחוֹב town square, marketplace (Pritz) (Gen 19:2)

Buildings

(For Roads, see Military ➨ Vehicles, Horses, and Travel ➨ Road)

(For Fortifications, see Military ➨ Fortifications)

General

בַּיִת house (1 Sam 25:1)

בְּנִיָּה a structure, building (Ezek 41:13 H)

בִּנְיָן edifice; structure, building (Hurvitz) (Ezek 40:5 R)

מִבְנֶה building (Ezek 40:2 H)

מִגְדָּל tower for military or agricultural purposes (Walsh); watchtower, platform (Pritz) (Isa 5:2)

מָלוֹן אֹרְחִים inn (Pritz) (Jer 9:2)

מִסְכְּנוֹת pillared or tripartite building (Borowski *Daily Life*); supply store, garrison (DCH) (1 Kgs 9:19 R)

פַּרְוָר summer house, treasury (DCH) (2 Kgs 23:11 R)

קִרְיָה building; town (Deut 2:36)

Royal/Palace

אַרְמוֹן citadel (1 Kgs 16:18)

בִּירָה palace; fortress, royal citadel, the temple (Hurvitz) (Esth 1:2)

בַּיִת palace (Pritz) (Gen 12:15)

בֵּית־הַמֶּלֶךְ palace (Pritz) (2 Sam 11:2)

בִּיתָן palace (Esth 1:5 R)

הֵיכָל palace (Pritz); temple; hall (1 Kgs 21:1)

הַרְמוֹן castle; high place (DCH) (Amos 4:3 H)

מִבְצָר fortification, fortress (DCH); fortress, stronghold, castle, citadel, fort (Pritz) (Hos 10:14)

מִסְגֶּרֶת panel, rim, stronghold (DCH) fortress, stronghold, castle, citadel, fort (Pritz) (2 Sam 22:46)

מְצָד   stronghold, mountain fastness (DCH); fortress, stronghold, castle, citadel, fort (Pritz) (Jer 51:30)

מָצוֹר   fortification, fortress (DCH) fortress, stronghold, castle, citadel, fort (Pritz) (Zech 9:3 R)

מִשְׂגָּב   stronghold (DCH); fortress, stronghold, castle, citadel, fort (Pritz) (2 Sam 22:3)

צְרִיחַ   citadel, crypt, underground chamber, vault (DCH); fortress, stronghold, castle, citadel, fort (Pritz) (Judg 9:46 R)

Temple

בִּירָה   palace; fortress, royal citadel, the temple (Hurvitz) (Esth 1:2)

דְּבִיר   inner sanctuary of temple (1 Kgs 6:19)

הֵיכָל   temple, palace, large public building; hall (2 Kgs 18:16)

מִקְדָּשׁ   sanctuary (Exod 15:17)

עֲזָרָה   court, enclosure of temple (Hurvitz); ledge, court (DCH) (2 Chr 4:9 R)

Prison

בּוֹר   prison; cistern (Gen 40:15)

בֵּית הָאֵסוּר   prison (SDBH) (Jer 37:15)

בֵּית הָאֲסִירִים   prison, dungeon (Pritz) (Judg 16:21 R)

בֵּית הַפְּקֻדֹּת   prison, dungeon (Pritz) (Jer 52:11 H)

בֵּית מִשְׁמָר   prison (Gen 42:19)

חָנוּת   prison, cell, vault (Jer 37:16 H)

כֶּלֶא   prison (1 Kgs 22:27)

כְּלִיא   prison; confinement (DCH) (Jer 37:4 H)

מַטָּרָה   jail, prison; target (Neh 3:25)

מַסְגֵּר   dungeon (Ps 142:8 R)

מִשְׁמָר   watch, imprisonment (Gen 40:3)

סֹהַר   dungeon; enclosure (DCH) (Gen 40:3 R)

עֹצֶר   prison, dungeon (Pritz) (Isa 53:8 R)

Storehouse

אוֹצָר   treasury, storehouse (Josh 6:19)

אָסָם   storehouse; grain store, silo (Pritz); grain pit (Borowski *Agriculture*); barn, granary (SDBH) (Deut 28:8 R)

אָסֹף   storehouse (Neh 12:25 R)

בֵּית הָאוֹצָר   storehouse, treasury (Hurvitz); storehouse; treasury; armory; granary; (wine) cellar (SDBH) (Mal 3:10)

גֶּנֶז   treasury (Hurvitz) (Esth 3:9 R)

גִּנְזַךְ   storeroom, treasury (Hurvitz) (1 Chr 28:11 H)

מַטְמוֹן   secret storehouse; treasure (DCH) (Gen 43:23 R)

מִסְכְּנוֹת   storagehouse, magazine (1 Kgs 9:19)

נְכֹאת   treasure house, treasury (SDBH) (2 Kgs 20:13)

פַּרְוָר   summer house, treasury (DCH) (2 Kgs 23:11 R)

Granary/Barn

אָסָם   storehouse; grain store, silo (Pritz); grain pit (Borowski *Agriculture*); barn, granary (SDBH) (Deut 28:8 R)

מַאֲבֻס   grain-store, silo (Jer 50:26 H)

מְגוּרָה   barn, granary; a fright; grain-store, silo; storehouse (Hag 2:19 H)

מְזָוִים   barns, storehouses, cells; barns, granaries (SDBH) (Ps 144:13 H)

מַמְּגֻרוֹת   granaries (DCH) (Joel 1:17 H)

מָעוֹג   round silo (DCH); cake, bread; loaf or slice of bread or cake (DCH) (1 Kgs 17:12 H)

קַרְקַע   barn; floor (DCH) (Num 5:17 R)

Tent

אֹהֶל   tent (Gen 4:20)

אַפֶּדֶן   pavilion, palace tent (Dan 11:45 H)

דּוֹר   dwelling (SDBH) (Isa 38:12 H)

חַוָּה   tent camp; tent village (DCH) (Num 32:41)

חֻפָּה   tent; canopy; pavilion (SDBH) (Ps 19:6 R)

יָתֵד   tent-peg, stake, nail, pin; peg on wall of house, for hanging objects (Pritz) (Exod 27:19)

סֻכָּה   vineyard booth (Walsh) (Isa 4:6)

מֵיתָר   tent rope; cord (Ps 21:13 R)

מִשְׁכָּן   tent (Pritz); tabernacle (DCH) (Num 24:5)

קֻבָּה   pavilion, tent, bedchamber (Num 25:8 H)

Structural Features

Entryway

אַיִל   gate, gateway (Pritz); pillar (DCH) (1 Kgs 6:31)

אַמּוֹת   doorposts (Pritz) (Isa 6:4 H)

דֶּלֶת   door, gate, lid (Gen 19:6)

מְזוּזָה   doorpost (Exod 12:7)

מִפְתָּן   threshold (1 Sam 5:4–5)

מַשְׁקוֹף   lintel, top beam of doorframe (Pritz) (Exod 12:7 R)

סַף   foundation, door, threshold, doorsill (Pritz) (Amos 9:1)

עָב   architrave (?), threshold (?); canopy (DCH) (1 Kgs 7:6 R)

פֶּתַח   opening door, entrance (Gen 4:7)

פֶּתַח הַשַּׁעַר   gate, gateway (Judg 18:16–17)

שַׁעַר   gate (Esth 2:19)

Door Locks/Bars/Hinges

בְּרִיחַ bar (Exod 26:28)

גְּלִילִים hinges (Pritz); hinged (DCH) (1 Kgs 6:34 R)

כַּפּוֹת הַמַּנְעוּל locks (Pritz) (Song 5:5)

מִפְתֵּחַ key (Pritz); connotation of authority (כְּלִי) (Judg 3:25 R)

נָעַל lock (Pritz) (Judg 3:23 R)

סָגַר to lock (Pritz) (Judg 9:51)

פֹּתוֹת hinges (Pritz); socket, secret parts (DCH) (1 Kgs 7:50 R)

צִיר hinge (Pritz) (Prov 26:14 H)

Stairs

לוּלִים stairs, steps (Pritz) (1 Kgs 6:8 H)

מַעֲלָה stair, step (Pritz) (Exod 20:26)

סֻלָּם stairway, steps (Pritz); ladder (DCH) (Gen 28:12 H)

Windows

אֲרֻבָּה lattice, window; chimney (Gen 7:11 R)

אֶשְׁנָב latticed window; window (DCH) (Judg 5:28 R)

חַלּוֹן window (Gen 8:6)

מֶחֱזָה window; light (1 Kgs 7:5 R)

צֹהַר window (Pritz); roof (DCH) (Gen 6:16 H)

שְׁקֻפִים windows (Pritz); window frame (1 Kgs 6:4 R)

Location

חוּץ outdoors (Lev 18:9)

פְּנִימָה indoors (2 Kgs 7:11)

Walls

גְּבוּל boundary wall, fence, boundary-marking stone (Pritz) (Ezek 40:12)

גָּדַר to build a wall or fence up (Pritz) (Job 19:8)

חוֹמָה boundary wall, fence (Pritz) (Lam 2:7)

חַיִץ boundary wall, fence (Pritz); interior wall; shaky wall (SDBH) (Ezek 13:10 H)

יָתֵד tent peg, stake, nail, pin; peg on wall of house, for hanging objects (Pritz) (Exod 27:19)

כֹּתֶל wall (of house) (Song 2:9 H)

מִגְרָעוֹת recesses, ledges (in wall) (1 Kgs 6:6 H)

מְשֻׂכָה boundary wall, fence (Pritz); hedge (DCH) (Prov 15:19 H)

קִיר boundary wall, fence (Pritz); wall, side, barrier (SDBH) (Ps 62:3)

שׂוּךְ to build a wall or fence up (Pritz) (Job 1:10 R)

שׁוּר wall (rich houses); boundary wall, fence (Pritz) (Gen 49:22 R)

Cornerstone/Capstone

אֶבֶן הָרֹאשָׁה	cornerstone, keystone, capstone (Pritz) (Zech 4:7)
אֶבֶן פִּנָּתָהּ	cornerstone, keystone, capstone (Pritz) (Job 38:6)
פִּנָּה	cornerstone, keystone, capstone (Pritz) (Zech 10:4)
רֹאשׁ פִּנָּה	cornerstone, keystone, capstone (Pritz) (Ps 118:22)

Rooms

בַּיִת	room (Pritz) (1 Chr 28:11)
גַּב	room (Pritz); back, brow, mound, platform for worship (DCH) (Ezek 16:24)
חֶדֶר	apartment, chamber (Gen 43:30)
חֶדֶר בְּחָדֶר	inner room with no outside windows (Pritz) (1 Kgs 20:30)
חֲדַר הַמִּטּוֹת	bedroom (Pritz) (2 Kgs 11:2)
חֶדֶר הַפְּנִימִים	inner rooms with no outside windows (Pritz) (1 Chr 28:11)
חֲדַר מִשְׁכָּב	bedroom (Pritz) (Exod 8:3)
חֻפָּה	bridal chamber, marriage bed (Pritz) (Joel 2:16 R)
יָצִיעַ	room; wing (of building) (HALOT); terrace (DCH) (1 Kgs 6:5 R)
לִשְׁכָּה	room; chamber (DCH) (1 Sam 9:22)
מַעֲלָה	upper room, roof chamber (Pritz) (Amos 9:6)
נִשְׁכָּה	chamber, temple cell (Neh 3:30 R)
סַף	vestibule; threshold (DCH) (Exod 12:22)
עֲלִיָּה	stairway; upper room (Ps 104:13)
צֵלָע	side chamber, cell (1 Kgs 6:5); plank, board (1 Kgs 6:16)
תָּא	chamber, guardroom (1 Kgs 14:28)

Cooking Area

מְבַשְּׁלוֹת	cooking hearths (Ezek 46:23 H)
מִקְטָר	hearth place; place of burning, incense altar (DCH) (Exod 30:1 H)

Floor/Foundation

מוֹסָד	foundations (Pritz); foundation, ruins, remains (DCH) (Deut 32:22)
מָכוֹן	foundation (Pritz) (Ps 104:5)
סַף	foundation, door (Pritz); threshold (DCH) (Amos 9:1)
קַרְקַע	floor (Num 5:17 R)
רִצְפָה	pavement, floor (Esth 1:6)

Roof

גֵּב	crossbeam, rafter (Pritz); trench; coffer, recess in paneled ceiling (DCH) (1 Kgs 6:9 R)
גַּג	roof (Deut 22:8)

דֶּלֶף　leaky roof (Prov 27:15 R)

כְּפִיס　girder, rafter; crossbeam (Pritz) (Hab 2:11 H)

מַעֲקֶה　parapet (Deut 22:8 H)

מְקָרֶה　roof, housetop (Pritz); beam-work, rafter (DCH) (Eccl 10:18 H)

זֵר　concave molding surrounding top of object or building, i.e., cavetto cornice (Eichler "The Meaning of Zçr"); border (DCH) (Exod 25:11)

סְפֻן　ceiling (1 Kgs 6:15 H)

קוֹרָה　rafter; roof; log, beam (DCH) (Gen 19:8 R)

קרה　to lay ceiling beams (Hurvitz) (Ps 104:3 R)

שְׂדֵרָה　roof; board; aligned beams (HALOT); row, plank (DCH) (1 Kgs 6:9 R)

Curtain/Screen

דֹּק　door of tent, dividing curtain (Pritz) (Isa 40:22 H)

יְרִיעָה　curtain, hanging (Ps 104:2)

מָסָךְ　curtain, screen (Exod 26:36)

פָּרֹכֶת　curtain (Exod 26:31)

קֶלַע　curtain, hanging (Exod 27:9)

Materials

גָּזִית　ashlar, hewn stone (1 Kgs 6:36)

טוּר　course, row (of ashlar or wood) (1 Kgs 6:36)

לְבֵנָה　brick (Exod 24:10)

מַלְבֵּן　brick kiln; brick pavement (SDBH) (Jer 43:9 R)

Boards/Planks

לוּחַ　board, plank (Exod 27:8)

קֶרֶשׁ　board, plank (Exod 26:15)

שָׂחִיף　board (planed) (Ezek 41:16 H)

Mortar

גִּר　chalk, lime (CT); plaster (Pritz) (Isa 27:9 H)

זֶפֶת　pitch, tar, asphalt (Isa 34:9 R)

חֵמָר　bitumen (Gen 14:10 R)

חֹמֶר　clay, "clay material used for pottery as well as mud plaster and mortar utilized for construction purposes" (Zhakevich) (Gen 11:3)

טִיחַ　mortar, plaster (Ezek 13:12 H)

שִׂיד　lime, whitewash (CT); quicklime plaster (Zhakevich); lime, mortar (DCH) (Isa 33:12 R)

תָּפֵל　plaster; frivolity; mud-based plaster unmixed with reinforcing elements (Zhakevich) (Ezek 13:10–15 R)

Enclosures

גֶּדֶר / גְּדֵרָה / גְּדֶרֶת   wall, stone fence (Num 22:24 R)

חָצֵר   court, enclosure (Exod 8:9)

רְחוֹב   plaza; square, street (DCH) (Neh 8:1)

Portico and Columns

אֶדֶן   pedestal, socket (Exod 26:25)

אוּלָם / אֵילָם   portico, porch (1 Kgs 6:3)

אַיִל   pilaster; pillar (DCH) (1 Kgs 6:31)

אֹמְנוֹת   columns; doorposts (Pritz) (2 Kgs 18:16 H)

דְּבִיר   column (Pritz); inner sanctuary, room (DCH) (2 Chr 3:16)

זָוִית   column (Pritz); corner (Hurvitz) (Psa 144:12 R)

כִּיּוֹר   platform (Pritz) (2 Chr 6:13)

כַּפְתּוֹר   capital of pillar; capital of column (Pritz); knob, ornament, capital of pillar (DCH) (Amos 9:1)

כֹּתֶרֶת   capital of column (Pritz) (Jer 52:22)

מִסְעָד   support pillar; balustrade; table, bench, bannister, support (DCH) (1 Kgs 10:12 H)

מָצוּק / מְצֻק   column (Pritz); pillar (DCH) (1 Sam 2:8 R)

עַמּוּד   column, stand, platform (Judg 16:25–26)

רֹאשׁ   capital of column (Pritz) (2 Chr 3:15)

Water Storage

בְּאֵר / בְּאֵר / בַּיִר   cistern; pit, cistern (DCH); well (Pritz) (Gen 16:14)

בְּרֵכָה   pool (Pritz) (2 Sam 2:13)

גֵּב / גֶּבֶא   well, cistern, keg; ditch for irrigation (DCH) (Jer 14:3 R)

מִקְוָה / מִקְוֶה   pool (Pritz); collection of water, reservoir (DCH); tank (SDBH) (Exod 7:19 R)

צִנּוֹר   water shaft, water tunnel, water channel, water supply (Pritz) (2 Sam 5:8 R)

Furniture

Couch/Bed

יָצוּעַ   bed, couch (Pritz) (Gen 49:4 R)

מִטָּה   bed, sofa; bier (Gen 47:31)

מֵסַב   bed, couch (Pritz); couch, surroundings (DCH) (Song 1:12 R)

מַצָּע   couch, bed (Isa 28:20 H)

מְרַאֲשׁוֹת   headrest; place of head, head support (DCH) (Gen 28:11)

מִשְׁכָּב   bed (Gen 49:4)

פְּעָמֹת   feet (of furniture) (Eichler "The Meaning of *Pa'am*") (Exod 25:12)

עֶרֶשׂ   couch, divan; bed (SDBH) (Deut 3:11)

Carpet, Rug

גֶּנֶז   carpet, rug (Pritz); treasure chest (DCH) (Ezek 27:24 H)

מַד   carpet, rug (Pritz); cloth, rug, garment (DCH) (Judg 5:10 H)

צָפִית   cloth, rug (SDBH) (Isa 21:5 H)

שְׂמִיכָה   carpet, rug (Pritz) (Judg 4:18 H)

Seat

אָבְנָיִם   birthstool (Pritz); stones (dual), pair of stones used as birthstool (DCH) (Exod 1:16 R)

כִּסֵּא   throne; chair, seat (Pritz) (Judg 3:20)

מוֹשָׁב   seat, chair (Pritz) (1 Sam 20:18 R)

מֶרְכָּב   seat; chariot (Song 3:10 R)

תְּכוּנָה   seat, chair (Pritz); fixed placer (DCH) (Job 23:3 R)

Footstool

הֲדֹם   footstool; metaphor for obeisence and submission (Salvesen "הֲדֹם") (Isa 66:1 R)

כֶּבֶשׁ   footstool (2 Chr 9:18 H)

Table/Storage

מֶלְתָּחָה   closet, cabinet, cupboard (Pritz); clothes, store, wardrobe (DCH) (2 Kgs 10:22 H)

מֵסַב   bed, couch (Pritz); table (DCH) (Song 1:12 R)

שֻׁלְחָן   table (Judg 1:7)

Lamps

לַפִּיד   lamp, torch; cresset (כלי) (Judg 7:16)

מָאוֹר   luminary, lightbearer (כלי) (Exod 27:20)

מְנוֹרָה/מְנֹרָה   menorah; lampstand (DCH) (2 Kgs 4:10)

נִיר/נֵר   lamp, light (Num 8:2)

פִּשְׁתָּה   flax (for linen, wicks); wick of a lamp, made of flax (כלי) (Exod 9:31 R)

CONTAINERS AND IMPLEMENTS

General Terms

חֶרֶשׂ   vessel made of cheap material (Pritz); pot, potsherd, earthenware (DCH) (Prov 26:23)

כְּלִי   vessel, implement, utensil, apparatus (Ruth 2:9)

צָמִיד   lid or cover (Kelso and Albright) (Num 19:15 H)

קֶרֶן   horn of animal used as container (SDBH) (1 Sam 16:1)

Chest/Box

אַרְגַּז   chest, box; bag (SDBH) (1 Sam 6:11 R)

אָרוֹן   box, chest, coffin (SDBH) (Gen 50:26)

Cup

גָּבִיעַ   goblet, calyx; pitcher (Kelso and Albright); special cup made of silver (Pritz) (Gen 44:12)

כּוֹס   cup; drinking vessel similar to bowl (Walsh); cup, purse (DCH) (2 Sam 12:3)

כִּיס   cup, bag (for money, weights); bag, purse (SDBH) (Deut 25:13 R)

קֻבַּעַת   goblet; small bowl (Kelso and Albright); cup, bowl, goblet (SDBH) (Isa 51:17 R)

קֶסֶת   cup, ink well; scribal palette (Zhakevich); writing case (DCH) (Ezek 9:2 R)

Crucible

מַצְרֵף   crucible (for silver) (Prov 27:21 R)

עֲלִיל   crucible, furnace (Ps 12:7 H)

Bowl, Basin

אַגָּן   bowl; large banquet bowl (Kelso and Albright) (Song 7:2 R)

אֲגַרְטָל   dish, bowl (SDBH); basket (DCH) (Ezra 1:9 R)

גֻּלָּה   basin, bowl (Eccl 12:6)

כִּיּוֹר   bowl (Kelso and Albright); basin for washing (DCH); cooking pot, kettle (Pritz) (Exod 30:18)

כְּפוֹר   bowl, basin; frost (1 Chr 28:17 R)

מִזְרָק   bowl, wine bowl, basin; bowl used for alcohol, ritual contexts (Walsh); shallow metal drinking-offering bowls (Greer); large banquet bowl (Kelso and Albright) (Amos 6:6)

מַחֲלָפִים   vessels of various kinds (Pritz); knives (DCH) (Ezra 1:9 H)

מְנַקִּית   sacrificial bowl (Exod 25:29 R)

סַף basin, goblet, bowl; vestibule; small bowl for sacrifice or wine (Kelso and Albright); cup (Pritz) (Zech 12:2 R)

סֵפֶל basin, bowl; large banquet bowl (Kelso and Albright); cup (Pritz) (Judg 15:25 R)

צְלֹחִית bowl (Kelso and Albright); jar (DCH) (2 Kgs 2:20 H)

קְעָרָה bowl, dish, platter (Exod 25:29)

רַחַץ wash basin (SDBH); washing (DCH) (Ps 60:10 R)

סִיר רַחַץ basin, washbasin (Pritz) (Ps 60:10)

מַשְׂרֵת bowl with perforated base, colander, strainer (FAJ); bread bowl for kneading dough (Kelso and Albright); pan, tray (DCH) (2 Sam 13:9 H)

Jug, Jar

אָסוּךְ oil jar (Kelso and Albright) (2 Kgs 4:2 H)

בַּקְבֻּק decanter (Kelso and Albright); jug (DCH) (1 Kgs 14:3 R)

דְּלִי pail, jar; bucket (SDBH) (Num 24:7 R)

כַּד earthenware jar, pail; jar for water or flour (Kelso and Albright) (Gen 24:14)

כִּירַיִם jar stand (Kelso and Albright); cooking furnace (DCH); double cooking stove (כלי) (Lev 11:35 H)

צִנְצֶנֶת vase, jar, pot (Exod 16:33 H)

קַשְׂוָה jug, jar (libations); flagon, pitcher (SDBH) (Exod 25:29 R)

Pot, Kettle

אָח firepot; brazier (כלי) (Jer 36:22 R)

דּוּד kettle, pot, basket; deep cooking pot (Kelso and Albright) (2 Kgs 10:7 R)

כּוּר smelting pot (for gold) (Prov 27:21 R)

כִּיּוֹן cauldron, chafing dish, fire pot; pedestal or palanquin (DCH) (1 Sam 2:14 H)

סִיר pot; thorn; hook; wide-mouth cooking pot, wash basin (Kelso and Albright) (Exod 16:3 R)

פָּרוּר cooking pot (Num 11:8 R)

קַלַּחַת kettle, cauldron, pot; stewpot (כלי) (1 Sam 2:14 R)

Pans

כַּף pan; palm of hand; ladle, spoon, saucer (DCH) (Exod 25:29)

מַחֲבַת pan, griddle, plate (Lev 2:5 R)

מַחְתָּה pan for live coals; firepan (DCH) (1 Kgs 7:50)

מַרְחֶשֶׁת baking pan, stove pan; cooking pan for deep-fat frying (Kelso and Albright); griddle (Pritz) (Lev 7:9 R)

צֵלָחַת shallow pan; medium sized bowl (Kelso and Albright); cooking pot, kettle (Pritz) (2 Kgs 21:13 R)

Flask

אָסוּךְ oil flask (2 Kgs 4:2 H)

בַּקְבֻּק flask, bottle; jug (SDBH) (1 Kgs 14:3 R)

פַּךְ flask, vial; small perfume juglet (Kelso and Albright) (1 Sam 10:1 R)

צַפַּחַת pilgrim flask, small oil jar (Kelso and Albright); clay jar (Pritz) (1 Sam 26:11 R)

קֶרֶן horn, flask (1 Sam 16:13)

Pottery

Formed Clay

חַרְסוּת potsherd, pottery (Jer 19:2 H)

חֶרֶשׂ pottery; earthenware vessel, clay pot (SDBH) (Lev 11:33)

כְּלִי יוֹצֵר potter's vessel (Kelso and Albright) (Ps 2:9)

עֶצֶב pottery vessel (?) (Kelso and Albright) (Jer 22:28 H)

Unformed Clay

אֲדָמָה land, soil (Gen 2:5); topsoil, humus (HCW); dry native clay (Kelso and Albright) (Isa 45:9)

אֶרֶץ earth, land; dry native clay (Kelso and Albright) (Ps 12:7)

חֹמֶר clay, "clay material used for pottery as well as mud plaster and mortar utilized for construction purposes" (Zhakevich) (Gen 11:3)

טִיט mud, mire, silt, clay (HCW) (Job 41:22)

עָפָר dust, raw clay (Kelso and Albright) (Job 10:9)

Oven

כִּבְשָׁן kiln, smelting furnace (Gen 19:28 R)

כִּיר stove, furnace (Lev 11:35 H)

תַּנּוּר oven, furnace, fire-pot (Lev 11:35)

Hearth

אֲרִיאֵל hearth (CHB) (Ezek 43:15 R)

יָקוּד hearth (CHB); glowing fire (כלי) (Isa 30:14 H)

מוֹקְדָה hearth (CHB) (Lev 6:2 H)

Sacks, Bags, Skins

אֹבוֹת wineskins, water bags (Pritz) (Job 32:19 H)

אַמְתַּחַת sack, bag; grain-storage bag carried by pack animals (כלי) (Gen 42:27)

חֵמֶת wineskin, water bag (Pritz) (Gen 21:14 R)

חָרִיט purse, bag (SDBH); wallet (Platt); purse (DCH) (2 Kgs 5:23 R)

יַלְקוּט (shepherd's) pouch, bag (SDBH) (1 Sam 17:40 H)

מֶשֶׁךְ leather bag, pouch (כלי) (Job 28:18 R)

מִשְׁפְּתַיִם saddlebags, donkey packs (כלי) (Gen 49:14 R)

נֹאד skin, bottle; made of animal skin (Walsh) (Josh 9:4 R)

נֶבֶל / נֵבֶל wineskin, jar, pitcher; large storage jar (Kelso and Albright); clay jar (Pritz) (Isa 30:14)

צִקְלוֹן satchel, saddlebag, sack, bag (2 Kgs 4:42 H)

צְרוֹר bundle, parcel, pouch; money pouch, purse (כלי) (Prov 7:20 R)

שַׂק sackcloth, bag (Isa 3:24)

Basket

אֵיפָה basket, specific measure of a basket (Pritz); tub, barrel (SDBH) (Lev 19:36)

דּוּד kettle, pot, basket; deep cooking pot (Kelso and Albright) (2 Kgs 10:7 R)

טֶנֶא basket (Deut 26:2 R)

כְּלוּב wicker basket (fruit); bird trap, cage (Jer 5:27 H)

סַל / סַלְסִלּוֹת bread basket, woven basket (Exod 29:3)

תֵּבָה basket (Pritz); ark (SDBH) (Exod 2:3)

Cutting Instruments

חֶרֶב sword, knife (Josh 5:2–3)

מַאֲכֶלֶת knife (eating); used to cut animal flesh (Koller) (Gen 22:6 R)

מַזְמֵרָה pruning knife (Joel 4:10 R)

מַחֲלָפִים slaughter-knives; specifically for ritual use in temple (Koller) (Ezra 1:9 H)

צֹר / צֻר knife, stone (flint) (Isa 5:28 R)

שַׂכִּין knife (Prov 23:2)

תַּעַר knife, razor; scabbard (Num 6:5 R)

Fork

מַזְלֵג fork (three-pronged) (Pritz) (1 Sam 2:13–14 R)

מַעֲצָד tongs (Pritz); axe, billhook (DCH) (Isa 44:12 R)

קִלְּשׁוֹן fork, points (Hurvitz) (1 Sam 13:21 H)

TOOLS

(Many other categories contain "Tools" vocabulary as well:
for Animal Husbandry Tools, see Animals ➡ Animal Husbandry Tools;
for Hunting Tools, see Animals ➡ Snares and Traps;
for Medical Tools, see Disease, Mortality, and Disability ➡ Medical Tools, Herbs;
for Harvesting Tools, see Food and Spices ➡ Threshing/Winnowing;
for Military Tools, see Military ➡ Weapons/Armor;
for Literacy, see Education ➡ Writing Tools and Implements)

General Tools

General

כְּלִי vessel, utensil, tool (כלי) (2 Sam 8:10)

מַטְאֲטֵא broom (Pritz) (Isa 14:23 H)

Rope/Cord/Ties

אֲגֻדָּה cord (SDBH); bond tying one to yoke (DCH) (Isa 58:6 R)

אַגְמוֹן rope, cord (Pritz); rush, used as barb (DCH) (Job 41:2 R)

חֶבֶל rope, cord (Pritz) (Job 18:10)

חוּט thread, cord (DCH) (Gen 14:23 R)

יֶתֶר cord; string; cord, sinew, tent rope, bowstring (DCH) (Judg 16:7 R)

לֻלָאָה loop (Exod 26:4)

מֵיתָר rope, cord (Pritz) (Exod 39:40 R)

מֹשְׁכוֹת ropes, cords (Pritz); belts (DCH) (Job 38:31 H)

נִקְפָּה rope (Isa 3:24 H)

עֲבֹת rope, cord, gold chains connecting ephod and shoulder straps on priestly garment (Pritz) (Exod 28:14)

פָּתִיל cord; thread (Gen 38:18)

Restraints/Chains

אֲזִקִּים chains, bonds, manacles (Jer 40:1 R)

אֵסוּר thong; strap; bond; fetter; cord; bond, fetter (DCH) (Judg 15:14 R)

זֵק chain; fetter (Job 36:8 R)

כֶּבֶל shackles, fetters, manacles (Pritz) (Ps 105:18 R)

מַהְפֶּכֶת stocks (Jer 20:2 R)

מוֹסֵר thong; strap; bond; fetter; cord; bond, fetter (DCH) (Job 39:5 R)

מַעֲדַנּוֹת chains (Pritz) (Job 38:31 R)

מֹשְׁכוֹת chains (Pritz) (Job 38:31 H)

נְחֻשְׁתַּיִם shackles, fetters, manacles (Pritz); bronze fetters (DCH) (Judg 16:21 R)

סַד   stocks (Pritz) (Job 13:27 R)

צִינֹק   iron collar; neck irons (Jer 29:26 H)

רַתּוּקוֹת   chains (Pritz) (1 Kgs 6:21 R)

Barber/Haircutting

מוֹרָה   razor (Pritz) (Judg 13:5 R)

תַּעַר   razor (Pritz) (Num 6:5 R)

Artisanal Tools

Textile Production

אֶרֶג   loom, shuttle of loom (Job 7:6 R)

Pottery

חוֹתָם   press mold (Kelso and Albright); seal, signet ring (DCH) (Job 38:14)

Hammer

הַלְמוּת   hammer, mallet (Judg 5:26 H)

לטשׁ   to hammer out, sharpen; to sharpen, whet, forge (DCH) (Gen 4:22 R)

מַסְמֵר / מַשְׂמְרוֹת   nail, peg; nail, perhaps scepter (DCH) (1 Chr 22:3 R)

מַקֶּבֶת   hammer (Judg 4:21 R)

מִקְשָׁה   hammered work (Exod 25:18 R)

פַּטִּישׁ   forge hammer (Isa 41:7 R)

רֶקַע   hammer (Pritz) (Num 16:38)

רקע   to hammer (DCH) (Ezek 6:11)

Carving/Writing

(For Writing Implements, see Education ➜ Writing Tools and Implements)

חֶרֶט   chisel (Zhakevich); stylus (Pritz) (Exod 32:4 R)

מְחוּגָה   compass; lathe (DCH); callipers (כלי) (Isa 44:13 H)

מִכְתָּב   writing, script, document, inscription (DCH) (Exod 39:30 R)

מִכְתָּם   inscription (DCH) (Ps 16:1 R)

מַקְצֻעָה   chisel, scraper; carpenter's knife, used for sharpening curved wood (Koller) (Isa 44:13 H)

מַרְצֵעַ   awl (Pritz) (Exod 21:6 R)

עֵט   iron or reed pen; for writing on hard surfaces, e.g. rock or metal (כלי) (Jer 17:1 R)

צִפֹּרֶן שָׁמִיר   emery point (Notebaart); hard stone tip of an עֵט (Zhakevich); stylus point (DCH); nail, tip of angle-tint tool (כלי) (Jer 17:1)

שֶׂרֶד   scribing-awl; chalk; tool used by a carpenter in the preparation of wood to be cut up (Zhakevich); marker, stylus (DCH) (Isa 44:13 H)

Saw

מְגֵרָה   saw; used for cutting stones (Koller); axe (DCH) (2 Sam 12:31)

מָשׂוֹר   saw, possibly carpenter's saw (Koller) (Isa 10:15 H)

Agricultural Tools

Axe

גַּרְזֶן   axe; axe, pickaxe, adze (DCH) (Deut 19:5 R)

כֵּילַף   axe, club, sledge hammer; crowbar (DCH); synonymous with קַרְדֹּם (Koller) (Ps 74:6 H)

כַּשִּׁיל   feller, axe, hatchet; smaller version of גַּרְזֶן used to chop wood (Koller) (Ps 74:6 H)

מַגְזֵרָה   cutting implement, blade, axe (2 Sam 12:31 H)

מַעֲצָד   axe; reaping tool, type of hoe (Borowski *Agriculture*); adze (Notebaart); used to carve and shape wood (Koller) (Isa 44:12 R)

קַרְדֹּם   axe; double-bladed, with axe on one side and adze on the other; used for chopping wood, pruning trees, and digging up plants and roots (Koller) (Judg 9:48 R)

Plow/Hoe/Farming/Harvesting/Threshing

אוֹפַן עֲגָלָה   wheel-thresher (Borowski *Agriculture*) (Isa 28:27)

אֵת   hoe, plowshare; generic digging tool (Borowski *Agriculture*); blade (DCH) (1 Sam 13:20 R)

גֹּרֶן   threshing floor (Borowski *Agriculture*) (Num 15:20)

חֶרְמֵשׁ   flint sickle (Borowski *Agriculture*) (Deut 16:9 R)

חָרוּץ   iron tooth for threshing sledge (Borowski *Agriculture*); threshing sledge (DCH) (Job 41:22 R)

יָתֵד   digging tool (Borowski *Agriculture*); peg, nail, digging stick (DCH) (Deut 23:14)

כְּבָרָה   sieve (Borowski *Agriculture*) (Amos 9:9 H)

מַגָּל   sickle (Pritz) (Joel 3:13 R)

מוֹרַג   threshing sledge (Borowski *Agriculture*) (Isa 41:15 R)

מַזְמֵרָה   pruning knife; pruning tool (Walsh); smaller than מַגָּל, specialized for pruning, especially grape vines (Koller) (Joel 4:10 R)

מִזְרֶה   winnowing fork (Borowski *Agriculture*) (Isa 30:24 R)

מַחֲרֵשָׁה   plowshare, pick-axe, mattock; possibly identical to מַעְדֵּר (Koller) (1 Sam 13:20–21 R)

מַטֶּה   threshing stick (Isa 28:27) (Borowski *Agriculture*); rod, club, shepherd's staff (Gen 38:18) (Pritz)

מַעְדֵּר   hoe (Isa 7:25 H)

נָפָה   sieve (Borowski *Agriculture*) (Isa 30:28 H)

רַחַת winnowing shovel (Borowski *Agriculture*) (Isa 30:24 H)

שְׁלֹשׁ קִלְּשׁוֹן fork for picking up piles of cuttings (Pritz) (1 Sam 13:21)

Mortar and Pestle

מְדֹכָה mortar (Num 11:8 H)

מַכְתֵּשׁ mortar (beaten out thing); hollow place (Prov 27:22 R)

עֱלִי pestle; crucible, cauldron (DCH) (Prov 27:22 H)

MEASUREMENT

General Terms

חֶבֶל	measuring line, rope (2 Sam 8:2)
חוּט	measuring tape, string (1 Kgs 7:15 R)
מַד	measure (Jer 13:25 R)
מִדָּה	tall; measure, size; tax (Lev 19:35)
מִסְפָּר	number (Deut 25:2)
מַתְכֹּנֶת	proportion, measurement, amount (Ezek 45:11 R)
פָּתִיל	measuring rod, measuring line (Pritz) (Ezek 40:3)
קַו	measuring line, measuring rod (DCH, Pritz) (Isa 28:17)
קָנֶה	measuring rod, measuring line (Pritz) (Ezek 41:8)
שָׁלִישׁ	threefold measure (Isa 40:12 R)
שַׂעַר	a measure (grain) (Gen 26:12 H)
תֹּכֶן	fixed quantity, measure (Ezek 45:11 R)

Liquid

כֹּר	*kor*-measure = 10 *baths* = 60 gallons (1 Kgs 5:2 R)
בַּת	*bath*-measure = 6 הִין (1 Kgs 7:26)
הִין	*hin*-measure = 3 קַב (Exod 29:40)
קַב	*qab*-measure = 4 לֹג (2 Kgs 6:25 H)
לֹג	*log*-measure = smallest unit (Lev 14:10 R)

Dry

כֹּר	*kor*-measure = 10 *ephahs* = 6.5 bushels (1 Kgs 4:22 R)
חֹמֶר	*homer* = 10 *ephahs*; about 220 liters or 6 bushels (SDBH) (Lev 27:16)
לֶתֶךְ	*letek*-measure = 5 *ephahs* (Hos 3:2 H)
אֵיפָה	*ephah*-measure = 20 quarts (Exod 16:36)
סְאָה	*seah*-measure = 1/3 *ephah*, equivalent to 7.3 liters or 7 quarts (SDBH); about 12 liters (DCH) (Gen 18:6 R)
קַב	*qab*-measure = 1/8 *ephah* (2 Kgs 6:25 H)
עֹמֶר	*omer*-measure = 2 quarts; heap, sheaf; 1/10 *ephah* (SDBH) (Exod 16:16 R)
עִשָּׂרוֹן	tenth-part (of *ephah*) (Lev 23:17)

Width

עֳבִי	thickness, width (1 Kgs 7:26 R)
רָחָב	width; wide (DCH) (Exod 3:8)
רֹחַב	width; breadth (DCH) (Gen 13:17)
רְחֹב/רְחוֹב	width; avenue; area (Gen 19:2)

Height

בָּמָה high place, height, *bamah*-altar (Num 21:28)

גֹּבַהּ elevated, powerful, arrogant; height (SDBH) (Gen 7:19)

מָרוֹם altitude, height (Jer 17:12)

נוֹף elevation; height; loftiness (SDBH) (Ps 48:3 H)

קוֹמָה height; stature (SDBH) (Gen 6:15)

רוּם height; hautiness (Prov 25:3)

רָמָה height, high place (1 Sam 22:6 R)

תָּלוּל high (SDBH) (Ezek 17:22 H)

Length

General

אֹרֶךְ length (Deut 30:20)

אָרֵךְ long (SDBH) (Ezek 17:3)

כִּבְרָה length, measure, distance; stretch of land (DCH)
(Gen 48:7 R)

Specific Lengths (Short to Long)

אֶצְבַּע finger ("inch") (Jer 52:21 H)

טֹפַח handwidth (Pritz) (Exod 25:25 R)

זֶרֶת hand-span (1/2 cubit) (Exod 28:16 R)

גֹּמֶד span, cubit (Judg 3:16 H)

אַמָּה cubit (18 inches) (Gen 6:15–16)

קָנֶה measuring rod of six cubits and a palm = 3.5 meters (Pritz)
(Ezek 42:18)

שָׂדֶה furrow length, about 20–30 meters (SDBH) (1 Sam 14:14)

צֶמֶד *tsamad*-measure = as much as what a yoke of oxen can plough
in a day, roughly an acre (DCH, Walsh) (Isa 5:10)

Weight

General

כֹּבֶד heaviness, weight, mass (Nah 3:3 R)

מִשְׁקוֹל weight (Ezek 4:10 H)

מִשְׁקָל weight, weighing (1 Kgs 10:14)

מִשְׁקֹלֶת / מִשְׁקֶלֶת weight, plummet; levelling implement (DCH) (2 Kgs 21:13 R)

Specific Weights (Light to Heavy)

גֵּרָה 1/20 shekel = *gerah*-weight, small weight (Exod 30:13 R)

בֶּקַע 10 gerahs = half-shekel, *beka*-weight (Gen 24:22 R)

פִּים 2/3 shekel = *pim*-weight (1 Sam 13:21 H)

שֶׁקֶל 2 bekas = shekel, weight (Gen 23:15–16)

מָנֶה 50 shekels = *mina*; measured amount (Ezek 45:12 R)

כִּכָּר 10 *minas* (75 lbs) talent (weight); load; circle, valley (Exod 25:39)

Currency

אֲגוֹרָה piece of silver (used as payment) (SDBH) (1 Sam 2:36 H)

אֲדַרְכּוֹן / דַּרְכְּמוֹן daric, drachma (SDBH) (1 Chr 29:7 R)

כֶּסֶף silver (Pritz) (Gen 13:2)

קְשִׂיטָה piece of money; coin; *kesitah* (SDBH) (Gen 33:19 R)

שֶׁקֶל shekel, currency (Gen 23:15 – 16)

Scales

אֶבֶן stone weight for scale (Pritz) (Lev 19:36)

כִּיס bag for money and weights (Deut 25:13 R)

מֹאזְנַיִם scales, balance (Lev 19:36)

פֶּלֶס balance, scale (Prov 16:11 R)

קָנֶה balance, scale (Pritz) (Isa 46:6)

APPENDIX ONE:
GUIDE TO FURTHER READING

Throughout our book, we note many specialized studies that cast light on difficult and rare terms. Here we wish to say a few words about the most relevant studies as they apply to the major categories and subcategories. In addition to the specific works discussed in this appendix, we note that probably the best place to start exploring semantic domains in Biblical Hebrew is the *Semantic Dictionary of Biblical Hebrew* (SDBH) project, sponsored by the United Bible Societies under the editorship of Reinier de Blois. The entire database is freely available online at sdbh.org. While some of the sources gathered in our book are written by specialists in lexicography and semantics, including those working on the Semantics of Ancient Hebrew Database project, others are written by archaeologists or literary scholars.

Heavens and Earth

For Hebrew cosmology and topography, the classic study is Stadelmann's *The Hebrew Conception of the World: A Philological and Literary Study*. On weather terms, see Scott, "Meteorological Phenomena and Terminology in the Old Testament," and, more recently, Wiggins's *Weathering the Psalms: A Meteorotheological Survey*.

Metals, Stones, Gems, Minerals, and Pearls

This area of research is in need of new work. SDBH is the best starting point by far. Brenner's *Colour Terms in the Old Testament* discusses some gems, while Notebaart's "Metallurgical Metaphors in the Hebrew Bible" contains the best (though still limited for our purposes) discussions of metallurgical terms.

Colors

The two key sources for this list are Brenner's *Colour Terms in the Old Testament* and Hartley's *The Semantics of Ancient Hebrew Colour Lexemes*. Each work offers unique elements and perspectives. Hartley's book, part of the Semantics of Ancient Hebrew Database project, is more current and covers each of its terms more in-depth. Brenner's book, however, integrates more terms that convey colour figuratively, such as jewels and textiles. She also includes evidence from Mishnaic Hebrew.

Time

A superb, comprehensive overview of time measurement in ancient Israel is Miano's *Shadow on the Steps: Time Measurement in Ancient Israel*. Dated and more theoretical, but still useful, is Barr's *Biblical Words for Time*.

Animals

Hope's *All Creatures Great and Small: Living Things in the Bible*, part of the UBS Technical Helps for Translators series, is the best place to start here. For animals that are kept for animal husbandry, Borowski's *Every Living Thing: Daily Use of Animals in Ancient Israel* and his *Agriculture in Iron Age Israel* are also a great help.

Flora

Our book separates cultivated plants from wild plants, placing the former under Food and Spices and the latter under Flora. On wild plants, Koops and Slager's *Each According to Its Kind: Plants and Trees in the Bible* is the single best resource available. Harrison discusses several plants as well in Healing Herbs of the Bible, though his book has some limits (see comments on this book under "Foods and Spices," below).

Human

Familial terms in the Hebrew Bible seem to be an understudied subject. The most useful works for this section were Eng's *The Days of Our Years: A Lexical Semantic Study of the Life Cycle in Ancient Israel*, which maps out age-related terms, and Parker's *Valuable and Vulnerable: Children in the Hebrew Bible*, which studies several different terms pertaining to children.

Human Anatomy

There is no English-language study of the semantics of human body parts in Biblical Hebrew. The most helpful source is Wilkinson, "The Body in the Old Testament," as well as two 2007 blog posts by Semitic linguist John Hobbins.

Disease, Mortality, and Disability

A useful place to start on diseases is Williams's "A Talmudic Perspective on Old Testament Diseases, Physicians and Remedies," though the subject has much room for further study. Harrison's *Healing Herbs of the Bible* lists many medicinal herbs and speculates on their specific use. On disability, Olyan's *Disability in the Hebrew Bible: Interpreting Mental and Physical Differences* is the best starting point, and Stewart's "Sexual Disabilities in the Hebrew Bible" covers sexual disabilities more specifically.

Foods and Spices

The best starting point for this subject is Koops and Slager's *Each According to Its Kind: Plants and Trees in the Bible*. Like the other books in the UBS Technical Helps for Translators series, this book contains vocabulary from both Testaments. On different types of crops and terms related to animal husbandry, Borowski's *Agriculture in Iron Age Israel* is superb, and it even includes an index of Hebrew terms. On herbs and spices, Harrison's *Healing Herbs of the Bible* is serviceable. Though light on textual analysis, he discusses some plants not mentioned in the Bible but only known from archaeology or comparative Near Eastern sources. For incense, see Nielsen's *Incense in*

Ancient Israel. On viticulture specifically, Walsh's *The Fruit of the Vine: Viticulture in Ancient Israel* is a thorough investigation incorporating both archaeological and textual data, with discussions of Hebrew terms throughout. While Walsh's book focuses on archaeology, Jordan's "An Offering of Wine," a 2002 dissertation, foregrounds semantic analysis of viticulture terminology. Two other books deserve mention. Nathan MacDonald's *What Did the Ancient Israelites Eat?: Diet in Biblical Times* is a highly readable guide to ancient Israelite diet. However, he does not discuss Hebrew terminology, making his book less useful for the Hebrew-language student. Kurtis Peters's *Hebrew Lexical Semantics and Daily Life in Ancient Israel: What's Cooking in Biblical Hebrew?* is a superb study of various terms for cooking activities.

Clothing

Like the metals and gems list, there is a surprising dearth of literature on this subject. SDBH and Pritz's *The Works of Their Hands: Man-Made Things in the Bible* are the best guides.

Family and Kinship

Almost no literature exists on familial terms in Biblical Hebrew. The best place to start, however, is Rattray's "Marriage Rules, Kinship Terms and Family Structure in the Bible."

Worship/Cultic

There are no guides to worship terminology in Biblical Hebrew. The best starting point is chapter 4, "Religion," in Pritz's *The Works of Their Hands: Man-made Things in the Bible.*

Law and Covenant

The main source here for legal terms is Bovati's *Re-Establishing Justice: Legal Terms, Concepts and Procedures in the Hebrew Bible.* On the language of oath, blessing, and cursing, see Aitken's *The Semantics of Blessing and Cursing in Ancient Hebrew,* published as part of the Semantics of Ancient Hebrew Database project.

Professions

There is no lexical study on professions overall in ancient Israel, although SDBH contains a category on "Professions" that is very useful. Apart from that, the terms for this must be gleaned from various studies on particular professions. For example, while Borowski's *Daily Life in Biblical Times* discusses different kinds of professions in the Old Testament, he seldom discusses specific Hebrew terms. His *Agriculture in Iron Age Israel* is useful, but only for terms relating to agricultural professions. There is no study on the terminology of political leadership in particular.

Military

For weapons, fortifications, and those engaged in war, see chapter 2, "Warfare," in Pritz's *The Works of Their Hands: Man-Made Things in the Bible.* On war in ancient

Israel more generally, see first Hobbs's *A Time for War: A Study of Warfare in the Old Testament*, and second, Seevers's *Warfare in the Old Testament: The Organization, Weapons, and Tactics of Ancient Near Eastern Armies*.

Maritime

Little exists on the terminology of seafaring in ancient Israel. Patai's *The Children of Noah: Jewish Seafaring in Ancient Times* is a good resource, which also includes Greek-language Jewish sources and Talmudic terminology. For a more focused examination of terminology in particular, see chapter 8, "Transportation," in Pritz's *The Works of their Hands: Man-Made Things in the Bible*.

Music

There is a large quantity of research into music in ancient Israel. The strongest guides to this subject integrate archaeological, textual (including non-biblical), and comparative ancient Near Eastern evidence on various musical instruments and those who played them. The most helpful resources for this category are Braun's *Music in Ancient Israel/Palestine: Archaeological, Written and Comparative Sources*, Burgh's *Listening to the Artifacts: Music Culture in Ancient Palestine*, and Montagu's *Musical Instruments of the Bible*.

Education

On terms relating to education in particular, see Van der Toorn's superb and readable *Scribal Culture and the Making of the Hebrew Bible*, which speculates on the social context of schools and scribes in ancient Israel. Widder's *"To Teach" in Ancient Israel: A Cognitive Linguistic Study of a Biblical Hebrew Lexical Set* is a more technical, linguistic study, focusing primarily on verbs but including some discussion of nouns related to education. On scribal tools in particular, see Zhakevich's dissertation "The Tools of an Israelite Scribe: A Semantic Study of the Terms Signifying the Tools and Materials of Writing in Biblical Hebrew," as well as Rollston's *Writing and Literacy in the World of Ancient Israel: Epigraphic Evidence from the Iron Age*.

Buildings and Structures

"Buildings and Structures," chapter 3 of Pritz's *The Works of Their Hands: Man-Made Things in the Bible*, is the main starting point for this topic. Borowski's *Agriculture in Iron Age Israel* details some of the buildings used in agriculture. His book has the advantage of including an index of Hebrew terms with glosses.

Containers and Implements

The best place to start here is Pritz's *The Works of Their Hands: Man-Made Things in the Bible*. Part of the UBS Technical Helps for Translators series, this book contains both Hebrew Bible and New Testament terminology. Another excellent starting point is Kelso and Albright's "The Ceramic Vocabulary of the Old Testament." Shafer-Elliot's article in *Biblical Interpretation*, "Food in the Hebrew Bible," is freely available online and contains many terms for implements used in cooking. The כלי *Database: Utensils in the Hebrew Bible*, an initiative of several Dutch biblical scholars, is far from comprehensive but boasts some very focused studies of the terms it does cover. Their results are freely available online.

Tools

Pritz's *The Works of Their Hands: Man-Made Things in the Bible* is the best starting point on biblical tools. The כלי *Database: Utensils in the Hebrew Bible*, an initiative of several Dutch biblical scholars mentioned above, is far from comprehensive but boasts some very focused studies of the terms it does cover. Their results are freely available online. For agricultural tools specifically, see Borowski's *Agriculture in Iron Age Israel* and Walsh's *The Fruit of the Vine: Viticulture in Ancient Israel*. On writing tools and materials, see Philip Zhakevich's recent dissertation, "The Tools of an Israelite Scribe: A Semantic Study of the Terms Signifying the Tools and Materials of Writing in Biblical Hebrew," freely available online in UT Austin Texas ScholarWorks. On cutting tools, see Koller's *The Semantic Field of Cutting Tools in Biblical Hebrew: The Interface of Philological, Semantic, and Archaeological Evidence*.

Measurement

As with the clothing list, there is also a surprising lack of literature on this subject. SDBH and Pritz's *The Works of Their Hands: Man-Made Things in the Bible* are the best places to start. Scott's "Weights and Measures of the Bible" also has some limited usefulness, though it is dated and he does not specifically discuss Hebrew terms. He does discuss some of the pitfalls in trying to "translate" biblical measurements into contemporary systems of measurement.

APPENDIX TWO:
CLUSTER VERSES FOR STUDY

Reading biblical vocabulary in contexts that are particularly revealing of a word's meaning can be quite helpful for memorization. We offer here a list of some of the more useful passages for this purpose. Cluster verses are individual verses or passages that contain several words from one category or subcategory. Memorizing these lists is a useful way to increase your Biblical Hebrew vocabulary, but these cluster verses enable you to learn these words in context. Some cluster verses are specific to a subcategory, while others are for a list overall. While the verses listed here are by no means exhaustive, we encourage students and instructors to use them as a model for developing their own examples and to email the authors with any cluster verses they may find.

I. The Created Order

Heavens and Earth: Gen 22:17; Deut 28:12, 32:22; Judg 5:4; 1 Sam 13:6;
2 Kgs 23:5; Ps 18:7–16, 29:7–9, 77:16–19, 83:13–15, 104:3, 135:7;
Prov 8:24–29; Job 38:22; Isa 29:6, 51:13–15; Jer 10:13, 17:6, 51:16;
Ezek 38:20–22

Stars: Job 9:9; Amos 5:8

Earth: Isa 40:4

Rain/Storm: Deut 32:2; Ps 65:10–11

Water: Exod 15:8; Ezek 31:4

Metals, Stones, Gems, Minerals, and Pearls: Gen 2:12; 1 Kgs 10:22

Metals: Exod 25:3; Num 31:22; Lam 4:1–2; Prov 27:21

Gems: Exod 28:17–20; Ezek 28:13

Specific Colors: Gen 30:32, 49:12; Exod 25:4, 26:31, 28:8, 35:6–7; Lev 13:19;
Isa 1:18; Zech 1:8, 6:2; Song 5:10–11; Lam 4:7–8; Esth 8:15

Time: Gen 7:11, 8:22; 1 Kgs 6:1, 6:37–38

Animals: Gen 15:9; Deut 14:4–6; Lev 11:1–8; 1 Sam 17:34; Song 1:8

Birds: Lev 11:13–19; Deut 14:11–18; Isa 34:15

Cattle: Gen 12:16; Job 1:3

Sheep, Goats: Gen 30:32–35

Horses, Mules, Asses: 1 Chr 27:30

Lions: Gen 49:9; Ezek 19:1–6; Nah 2:12

Lizards/Reptiles: Lev 11:29–30

Snakes: Deut 32:33; Isa 14:29

Arthropods: Lev 11:22–23

Locusts: Joel 1:4
Snares and Traps: Job 18:8–10
Flora: Num 24:6; Judg 8:9–15; 2 Kgs 19:26
Trees: Gen 30:37; Lev 23:40; Neh 8:15; Song 1:17; Isa 41:19, 44:14; Hos 4:13; Ps 45:9
Reeds: Exod 2:3
Flowers and Plants: Song 2:1
Parts of Trees and Plants: Gen 1:11; Lev 23:40; Isa 11:1

II. The Human Order

Human: Lev 21:13–14
Human Anatomy: Lev 13; Song 4:1–5
Disease, Mortality, and Disability: Lev 13, 21:18–21, 26:16; Num 5:2; Deut 15:21
Disabilities: Exod 4:11; Lev 19:14; Deut 23:1, 28:28; 2 Sam 5:8
Food and Spices: Deut 8:8; 2 Sam 17:27–29; 2 Kgs 4:39, 18:31–32; Mic 6:15; Song 1:10–14, 6:11
Grains: Exod 9:31; Ezek 4:9
Grain: Baked Goods/Dough/Leaven: Lev 23:17; Isa 28:24–29
Vine, Wine, Grapes (includes Strong Drink): Gen 49:11–12; Prov 23:30–31; Isa 5:1–4, 16:10; Jer 2:21, 48:32–33; Mic 7:1
Dairy: Judg 5:26
Fruits: Num 13:23; Joel 1:12
Vegetables: Num 11:5
Herbs and Spices: Gen 37:25; Exod 30:23–25
Jewelry: Num 31:50; Isa 3:18–23
Fabric: Esth 1:6

III. The Social Order

Immediate Family: Lev 18:6–18
Worship/Cultic: 1 Kgs 7
Ark of the Covenant: Exod 25:10–22
Menorah/Lampstand: Exod 25:31–39
Garb (Priestly): Exod 28:4, 28:39
Accoutrements: 1 Kgs 7:41–45, 7:48–50
Vow: Num 30:5
Idolatry: Lev 26:1
Divination: Exod 28:30; Deut 18:10; 1 Sam 28:3
Law and Covenant: Gen 20:5, 31:36; Exod 23:6–7; Lev 5:1, 19:15; Deut 16:18–20, 19:15–19, 25:1–2; 1 Sam 24:15; 2 Sam 15:4
Professions and Occupations: 1 Sam 8:13
Merchants/Business/Banking: Isa 23:8

Military: Num 31:14; 1 Sam 17:4–7; 1 Chr 14:7–8; Jer 51:20–21
Vehicles, Horses, and Travel: 1 Kgs 7:33; 1 Sam 8:11
Spoils, Plunder, Booty: Num 31:10–12
Maritime: Ezek 27:4–9, 27:25–30; Jonah 1:4–6
Music: Gen 4:21; Exod 15:20; 1 Sam 10:5, 18:6; 2 Sam 6:5; 1 Kgs 1:39–41; 1 Chr 16:5, 25:1; Pss 33:2, 68:24–25, 81:2–3, 150:3–5; Isa 5:12, 24:8; Amos 5:23, 6:5
Writing Tools and Implements: Jer 36:18; 36:23

IV. The Constructed Order

Buildings and Structures: 1 Kgs 6:3–6, 7:1–22; Ezek 13:14
Containers and Implements: Judg 6:19
Pottery: Lev 11:33–35
Artisanal Tools: 1 Kgs 6:7; Isa 44:12–13; Judg 5:26
Agricultural Tools: 1 Sam 13:20–21
Dry Measurement: Ezek 45:11

HEBREW WORD INDEX

SCRIPTURE INDEX